D1453492

Presented to

_____

By

_____

On the Occasion of

_____

Date

_____

GOD
CALLING

A Timeless Classic
Updated in Today's Language

EDITED BY
Lacie Stevens and Patti Velasquez

Whitecaps Media
HOUSTON

Whitecaps Media
Houston, Texas
whitecapsmedia.com

God Calling: A Timeless Classic Updated in Today's Language

ISBN-13: 978-0-9836825-9-2

Cover designed by Stephanie W. Dicken. Cover photo by Paul Paladin via Pond5.com.

Main body composed in Minion Pro 10/13.

Lacie Stevens and Patti Velasquez may be contacted through the publisher's website.

Printed in the United States of America

2   3   4   5   6   7   8

CONTENTS

INTRODUCTION

God is calling. To each of us. Each and every day. Hearing from Him on a daily basis is as vital today as it was when our Lord Jesus commanded His disciples: "Follow Me" (Matthew 4:19).

As you meditate on these pages, you will hear how much God loves you and how He longs to have a close, personal relationship with you. You will hear His sweet assurance that He is always with you (September 1); that there is nothing you can do to make Him love you any more—and nothing you can do to make Him love you any less.

Learn that what you have been searching for is Him (December 9). Hear His promise that He is your refuge (September 7), your strong tower. He is your hope (November 19), your provider (September 2), and your guide (March 26). He is everything you need.

This book is a collection of messages our Lord spoke to two anonymous women known only as the "Two Listeners" who spent time each day seeking to hear His call. To paraphrase the book's first editor, we did not write this book. We are simply two of the many people who, for years, have been blessed to spend time reading and reflecting on the beauty of those messages.

The Two Listeners consented to have their volume published "to prove that a living Christ speaks to-day, plans and guides the humblest, that no detail is too insignificant for His attention, that He reveals Himself now as ever as a Humble Servant and Majestic Creator." The original editor, A. J. Russell, prepared the volume for publication confident that the Lord opened the eyes of the Two Listeners "to many things which they and this generation greatly need to know."

And this generation's greatest need is to know that Jesus is not a distant god, but a personal God and Savior. He does not invite us to have religion. He invites us to have that close, personal relationship.

This devotional bears eloquent witness to that central truth. It contains many messages that our generation and generations to come need to know. Yet, as each of us read the messages slowly and carefully in our daily quiet time, we were troubled by the possibility that the truth and beauty contained in the devotionals were obscured by the language and syntax which were used. Although the writing may have been quite clear when the book was written eighty years ago in England, the now-outdated style had become archaic and sometimes confusing.

Eventually, each of us felt called by God to rewrite *God Calling* to clarify it and update it in the same way James Reimann edited *My Utmost for His Highest* by Oswald Chambers. With no small amount of hesitation, we shared with one another that we felt God was calling each of us to this task. It was a call for both of us to work together just as the Two Listeners had. Jesus taught about the power of two people working together.

Our friendship has its roots in service and obedience. It is God-ordained, Christ-centered, and Spirit-filled. Our deepest desire was and is to love and follow and serve Him. When we are together and meet others, we want them to know that Jesus is the Divine Third in our friendship (see May 11).

Thus began our six-year journey. The task was accepted with awe and reverence. We were and are humbled by the trust God placed in us to rewrite what is one of the most beloved devotionals of all time. We felt as if the Lord had handed us the Hope Diamond and said, "Now make it more brilliant still!"

So how do you approach such a high calling? We did it with hundreds and hundreds of hours of prayer and praise and worship. Our first writing session was preceded by eight hours of preparation consisting of prayer, confession, and praising and worshiping God in song. To this very day as we make the final changes, praying always precedes working.

Our fervent prayer was that we would be totally surrendered to God. We prayed that He would be completely in charge of the process and write through us. When we got impatient with our seemingly slow progress, He would gently remind us that His timing is perfect. Frequently, the day's devotional we were working on was one we could not fully understand except for the experience one of us had just been through. We drew so close to our Savior by spending hour after hour with Him and these beautiful messages. We wept over what He was able to accomplish through us as He unpacked the meaning of what had been hard to read and understand. He transformed our hearts, renewed our minds, and refreshed our spirits as we co-labored with Him to bring this precious volume up to date. He has etched the messages so deeply into us. No one has been more blessed by this book than we have been.

God laid down several principles to guide us in our work. First, He directed us to make the messages abundantly clear to everyone. These messages are truly gems that you can take into yourself, and they change you from the inside out. You will "taste and see that the LORD is good" (Psalm 34:8 NIV 1984).

Second, God impressed on us the necessity to not change the meaning of the original messages in any way. To that end, we have included portions of the devotionals which are often omitted from on-line or print versions of the book. We pray that our handling of the devotionals have not left our fingerprints on them at all. We have also included the original introductions ("The Two Listeners" and "The Voice Divine") as they first appeared, without revision.

Third, God convicted us of the importance of leading people to read their Bibles, because so many of the messages contain or are based on Scripture. The Scripture references have been added so that readers can go directly to God's Word. The translation which best suited the day's message has been quoted, but you can look up passages in any version of the Bible you use. Hopefully, as you read this book, you will find yourself putting it down often to open up your Bible.

Lastly, and most importantly, God is calling you to draw closer to Him and His Word. This book does not speak with the authority of Scripture. It is not a destination; it is a sign pointing you heavenward. It is not a book of prophecy or prediction, nor a horoscope disguised as Christian writing. It is a means to draw you nearer to the God who loves you, cares about every detail of your life, and longs for your friendship. He is calling to you today. May you have eyes to see and ears to hear.

BLESSINGS,
Lacie and Patti
September 2012

THE TWO LISTENERS

Idid not write this book. I wish that I had done so.

Had I written it I should have been immeasurably proud. Too proud for spiritual health.

My simple task has been to prepare it for publication and to present it to the public. But that has not really been a task — only a privilege; an undeserved honour.

There is a legend that the praise for building the Cathedral of St. Sophia was not given to the Emperor Constantine but to Euphrasia, a poor widow who drew from her mattress "a wisp of straw and gave it to the oxen" that drew the marble from the ships. That was all, she did nothing more.

Not one woman but two have written this book; and they seek no praise. They have elected to remain anonymous and to be called "Two Listeners." But the claim which they make is an astonishing one, that their message has been given to them, to-day, here in England, by The Living Christ Himself.

Having read their book I believe them.

I do not of course believe that He whispered to them all that He intends to say to this generation. But I am confident that He opened their eyes to many things which they and this generation greatly need to know.

I do not believe in the verbal inspiration of this or any book. But I do believe that these two women have been led and that much of what is written is very clear leading indeed.

I have found these messages a spiritual stimulus. But that statement is as inadequate as to say that I like England. None could have written this book unless he or she was a Christian and in touch with the Living Founder of Christianity.

We hear much of the decline of the drama. Think of this piece of real drama, of our own times. Again, as so often before, "He was in the world and the world knew Him not."

Two poor, brave women were courageously fighting against sickness and penury. They were facing a hopeless future and one of them even longed to be quit of this hard world for good. And then He spoke. And spoke again!

Day after day He comes and cheers them. And though they still have their sorrows they have joy and a new courage. For He inspires them with His promises for their future when His loving purpose shall be revealed; and He gently rallies them on their unbelief, as He did their forlorn predecessors during that walk to Emmaus.

Open this book at any page and taste its beauty. Dwell lovingly on its tender phrases. Let its wonderful quality sink deep into your spirit.

Have you lost faith? Meditate on any one of these tiny sections and it will come again to you as that of a little child. You may not see Him standing by your side with His ready smile of confident encouragement; but you will know that He is there, as He always is, and that He still expects great things of you, and is ever ready to help you to achieve them.

If winter comes are you afraid of poverty? Turn again to these pages and you will find the law of supply — Give and it shall be given you. Give your love, your time, your sympathy, yourself; give all that you have under His direct guidance to all who are needy; give both to the deserving and the undeserving.

Has health gone? Are you no better though you have prayed long and often? Here again you will find the incense of healing; and you will understand why He will not remove the gold from the crucible until all the dross has gone, and you are taking the glorious shape of your true self which His eye alone has foreseen.

You cannot eat honey all the day. Nor can you read this book through at a sitting. But you can read it every day, and several times a day.

It can be turned to in the heat of a sudden crisis, and when you put it down you will find yourself calm and at peace within.

You can open its pages when the birds are singing in the sunshine; and as you read, the song of the birds will be echoed in your spirit, for you too will be carolling your love to our Creator-Redeemer.

Put this book of "Daily Power" in your pocket, in your handbag, on the table by your bedside. Give a copy of it to your friends.

Inhale its spirit continually and live your life in its intimacy with The Master.

Through this message, which came to two lonely women, you will find that you are no longer one and alone, but two and united with The Great Companion and Guide, Who is the same yesterday, to-day, and for ever.

A. J. Russell

IF TWO AGREE ...

*If two of you agree on earth concerning
anything that they ask, it will be done for
them by My Father in heaven.*

*For where two or three are gathered
together in My name, I am there
in the midst of them.*

MATTHEW 18:19–20 (NKJV)

THE VOICE DIVINE

BY ONE OF THE "TWO LISTENERS"

In the autumn of 1932, I was sitting in the lounge of an hotel when a visitor, quite unknown, crossed over and, handing me a copy of *For Sinners Only*, asked if I had read it. I answered "No," and she left it with me.

On returning home, I bought a copy for myself.

I was curiously affected by the book and felt that I wanted all my friends to read it immediately, and actually made out a list of over a hundred people to whom I should have liked to have sent it. Not being rich, this desire had to be content with two copies, which I lent to various people, on whom it seemed to make little effect.

A few months later I read it again. It was then that there came a persistent desire to try to see whether I could get guidance such as A. J. Russell reported, through sharing a quiet time with the friend with whom I was then living. She was a deeply spiritual woman with unwavering faith in the goodness of God and a devout believer in prayer, although her life had not been an easy one.

I was rather skeptical, but, as she agreed, we sat down, pencils and paper in hand and waited. This was in December 1932.

My results were entirely negative. Portions of texts came and went, then my mind wandered to ordinary topics. I brought it back again and again, but with no success. To this day, I cannot get guidance in this way alone.

But with my friend a very wonderful thing happened. From the first, beautiful messages were given to her by our Lord Himself, and every day from then these messages have never failed us.

We felt all unworthy and overwhelmed by the wonder of it, and could hardly realize that we were being taught, trained, and encouraged day by day by HIM personally, when millions of souls, far worthier, had to be content with guidance from the Bible, sermons, their Churches, books and other sources.

Certainly we were not in any way psychic or advanced in spiritual growth, but just very ordinary human beings, who had had more suffering and worry than the majority and who had known tragedy after tragedy.

The tender understanding of some of Our Lord's messages was at times almost heart-breaking: but His loving reproofs would leave no hurt.

Always, and this daily, He insisted that we should be channels of Love, Joy and Laughter in His broken world. This was the Man of Sorrows in a new aspect.

We, or rather I, found this command very difficult to obey, although to others it might have been simple. To laugh, to cheer others, to be always joyful when days were pain-racked, nights tortured by chronic insomnia, when poverty and almost insupportable worry were our daily portion, when prayer went unanswered and God's face was veiled and fresh calamities came upon us?

Still came this insistent command to love and laugh and be joy-bringers to the lives we contacted.

Disheartened, one of us would gladly have ceased the struggle and passed on to another and happier life.

But He encouraged us daily, saying that He would not break the instruments that He intended to use, that He would not leave the metal in the crucible longer than was necessary for the burning away of the dross. Continually He exhorted us not to lose heart, and spoke of the joy that the future held for us.

Totally unexpected interpretations of His own words were given.

An adverse verdict on seeing visions of Himself, which we had hitherto thought granted only to the saintliest and, most strongly stressed of all, the immense power given to *two* souls praying together in close union and at one in their desire to love and serve Him. As others have proved, "such a union may, in God's hands, accomplish such great things that there certainly will be inimical forces whose purpose is to mar the friendship." And so we found it.

Some of the messages are of surprising beauty. The majestic language of December 2nd, the inevitability of suffering in the Christian Life of November 23rd, and the explanation of the practical working of the Law of Supply of December 5th are examples of this.

Others may appear disjointed. This is because personal references and repetition have had to be deleted.

So to us this book, which we believe has been guided by our Lord Himself, is no ordinary book.

It is published, after much prayer, to prove that a living Christ speaks to-day, plans and guides the humblest, that no detail is too insignificant for His attention, that He reveals Himself now as ever as a Humble Servant and Majestic Creator.

JANUARY 1
BETWEEN THE YEARS

*Our Lord and our God, we rejoice in
You. Without Your help, we could not
face the year ahead of us unafraid.*

I stand between the years. The light of My presence is already spread over the year to come, the
radiance of the sun of righteousness. My shadow is
cast over the year that lies behind, hiding trouble
and sorrow and disappointment.

Do not dwell on the past. Concentrate only on
the present. Only use the past in the same way that
trees use My sunlight. They absorb it, so that when
they are put in the fire in the days ahead, others are
warmed by My light which is then released. That
is how you must store the blessings from Me, the
Light of the world. Be encouraged by the knowledge that the blessings of the past will be released
in the days ahead to warm others.

Bury every fear: fear of the future, fear of poverty for yourself or those dear to you, of suffering,
of loss. Bury every thought of unkindness and bit-
terness, all of your dislikes, all of your resentments,
your sense of failure, your disappointment in others

and yourselves, your sadness, your hopelessness. Let us leave them all, buried, and go forward to a new and risen life.

Remember that you must not see things as unbelievers see them. I hold the year in My hands—and I hold it in safekeeping for you. But I shall only guide you and reveal it to you one day at a time.

Receive this year as you live each day, and leave the rest of it with Me. You must not anticipate the gift of this year with fears or questions about what may lie ahead.

I will supply the wisdom and the strength for each day.

JANUARY 2
ARM OF LOVE

You are meant to help save others. Don't let one day pass without reaching out an arm of love to someone outside your home—a note, a letter, a visit, or help in some way.

Be full of joy. Joy saves. Joy cures. Rejoice in Me. Look for the joy in every ray of sunlight, every smile, every act of kindness or love, and every act of service, no matter how small.

Every day, do something to lift another soul out of the sea of sin, or disease or doubt into which mankind has fallen. Even today, I continue to walk by the lakeside and call My disciples to follow Me and to become fishers of men (Matthew 4:19). You must lend your helping hand to those in need in order to give them courage and strength for the battle, to encourage their faith and to restore them to health. Love. Laugh. Love and laughter draw us to faith and courage. Trust and keep on trusting! Love and keep on loving! Rejoice and keep on rejoicing!

Refuse to be depressed. Refuse to let anything keep you from climbing higher. Love and laugh. I am with you. I carry your burdens. Give Me your burdens to carry, and I will keep you from falling. You will find yourself so lighthearted that you will then be able to help others weighed down with burdens too heavy for them to carry alone.

How many burdens can you lighten this year? How many hearts can you cheer up? How many souls can you help?

Remember My teaching that in giving, you also receive: "Give, and it will be given to you. A good measure, pressed down, shaken together and running over" (Luke 6:38 NIV 1984). I, your Lord, have said it.

JANUARY 3
I WILL MAKE THE WAY

"But those who hope in the LORD
will renew their strength."
(ISAIAH 40:31 NIV 1984)

You must be renewed, remade. Jesus, Jesus, Jesus. Everything must rest on Me, have its foundation in Me. Power comes from rest. Only love is a conquering power. Don't be afraid. I will help you.

I am calling you both to be channels. When you are unblocked channels, My Holy Spirit will flow through you and, in flowing through, will sweep away all of the pain of your past.

Be encouraged. God loves, God helps, God fights, God wins. You will see these truths. You will know these truths. I will go before you on the path to make the way. Everything My love has ever planned, everything My love has ever thought, you shall see unfold each day. Only you must be like a child, willing to be taught. Children never question plans. They accept them gladly.

JANUARY 4
DO NOT PLAN

"Show [us] Your ways, O Lord;
teach [us] Your paths.
Lead [us] in Your Truth and teach [us] ..."
(PSALM 25:4–5A NKJV)

All is well. Wonderful things are happening. Do not limit Me in any way. I care for you and provide for you.

Rid yourself of "self." It is "self" which prevents you from being unblocked channels. Do not plan ahead. I will only reveal the path to you one step at a time. Don't try to carry tomorrow's burden today. I am the great burden-bearer. You cannot bear My load. And I only expect you to carry a small backpack of today's concerns.

JANUARY 5
HOARD NOTHING

Love Me, and do My will. No evil will come against you. Do not worry about tomorrow. Resting in My presence brings peace. I will help you.

I will give you "the desires of your heart" (Psalm 37:4 NIV 1984). You will experience peace which, like a quiet, flowing river, cleanses and sweeps away every irritation.

You are being taught. Continue to spend time in prayer even if you do not see the results of your prayers at once. Satan will use any way he can to try to keep you from praying. Don't pay any attention to him! Satan will say evil spirits will enter into you. Don't pay any attention to him!

Relax. When you are in trouble, be at peace. If you act upset, those who see you will think that the God you worship is not able to deliver you. If you remain calm, you give bold witness to My power. Hope all the time.

Do not be afraid of poverty. Let money flow freely. I will let it flow in, but you must let it flow out. I do not send money to those who would hold onto it greedily for themselves. Rather, I send money only to those who pass it on. Keep nothing for yourself. Hoard nothing. Only have what you need and will use. This is My law of discipleship.

JANUARY 6
SHARP AND READY

"Guide me, O Thou great Jehovah,
Pilgrim through this barren land.
I am weak but Thou art mighty,
Guide me with Thy powerful hand."
("GUIDE ME, O THOU GREAT JEHOVAH,"
WILLIAM WILLIAMS, 1745)

You must pray. I will make the way. I care for you and I will reveal My plans to you. Just love and wait.

Love is the key. There is no door that is too difficult for love to open.

What reason do you have to be afraid? Haven't I always cared for you and protected you? Keep hoping. Hope gladly. Hope with certainty. Be calm, calm in My power.

Always find time to pray and read your Bible. You must train and discipline yourself. That is your job. It is then My job to use you. My instruments must be sharp and ready before I can use them.

Discipline and perfect yourselves at all costs. When you are obedient in doing this, all of your prayers will be answered. "I will give you the desires of your heart (Psalm 37:4 NIV 1984)," and I will use every act for My glory. It is an awesome power, a mighty power. Therefore, be careful that you do not ask for anything that is not in accordance with My Holy Spirit.

All negative thoughts must be forced out. In the wrong hands, miracle-working power can become witchcraft. The purity and goodness of your lives is essential. Soon, you will ask and the answer will come at once. Welcome the training. I do not dare give you this power unless you have been trained.

Do not worry about others' lives. Leave them to Me, for I will work everything out. You must perfect yourselves first in My strength.

JANUARY 7
THE SECRET PEARL

Look upon us with Your favor, O Lord, while we behold heaven, "the land that is very far off" (Isaiah 33:17 NKJV) and yet so near to the one who has "eyes to see and ears to hear" (Matthew 13:16 NIV 1984).

Wait. Wonders are unfolding. Tremble with awe. No one can stand at the doorway to eternity without shaking. I give you eternal life. A free gift. A wonderful gift. Life everlasting.

The kingdom of God comes silently. No one knows when a person accepts Jesus into his heart. It only becomes clear from their words and actions. Listen quietly for Me to speak to you. Sometimes you may get no message. Even when you do not hear Me speak, keep meeting with Me anyway. You will feel Me being there with you, and find yourself in a holy place not made of walls but made of My presence.

Practice silence. I speak in silences. Silence or a soft wind can each be a message to reveal My meaning to your heart. I do not need to use a voice — or even a word — to speak to you.

Each word or thought of yours can be like a pearl that you drop into the secret place of another's heart. In an hour of need, that person suddenly finds the treasure, and realizes its value for the very first time.

Don't be so eager to "do." Just "be." I said, "Be perfect" (Matthew 5:48 NIV 1984), not do perfect things. Try to understand this. Your effort alone will achieve nothing. It is only the work of the Holy Spirit, My Spirit, that counts.

Spend more and more time thinking about these truths. My followers have taken a lifetime to understand them.

JANUARY 8
LOVE CLOSES DOORS

Life with Me is not immunity from difficulties, but peace in difficulties. Many times I will guide you by closing doors to paths I do not want you to follow. My loving hand closes some doors as well as opens others.

Joy is the result of faithful, trusting acceptance of My will, even when it does not seem joyful.

My servant, the Apostle Paul, learned this lesson of the closed doors when he said, "These troubles and sufferings of ours are, after all, quite small and won't last very long. Yet this short time of distress will result in God's richest blessing upon us forever and ever!" (2 Corinthians 4:17 TLB).

Expect rejection until this lesson is learned. It is the only way.

Joy is the daughter of calm.

JANUARY 9
NO STRESS

Be calm, no matter what happens to you. Rest in Me. Be patient, because being patient will bring wonderful results in your life. "Patience develops strength of character in us and helps us trust God more each time we use it until finally our hope and faith are strong and steady" (Romans 5:4 TLB). Never be overwhelmed. How can you be overwhelmed when I am with you?

Do not feel the stress of life. My children have no reason to worry. Don't you realize that I am a master instrument-maker? Didn't I make every part? Don't I know the limits of what each instrument can bear without strain? Would I, the maker of such a delicate instrument, ever ask anything of it that would harm it or destroy it?

No! As My instruments in this world, you only experience stress when you are serving another master (the world, fame, what people think of you) or are trying to carry two days' burden on one day.

Remember, you must not do this.

JANUARY 10
INFLUENCE

When you come to Me, and I give you that eternal life I give to everyone who believes in Me, it alters your whole existence, including every word that you speak and every influence you have.

The words you speak and the influences that you have on others are eternal. They must be. They come from My life within you, "a spring of water welling up to eternal life" (John 4:14 NIV 1984). Therefore, they also live forever. Now you can see how immense, how amazing, is the work of any soul who has eternal life. The words, the influences, go on down through the ages forever.

You must spend time in serious thought on these truths I give you. These are not shallow observations; these are the deep things about Me and My kingdom that are vital to your being Mine. They are hidden pearls of great price (Matthew 13:45–46).

Continue to pray about and consider these truths. Work at them in your hearts and minds.

JANUARY 11
THE PAIN OF LOVE REJECTED

Cry out to Me, and I will hear you and bless you. Use My unlimited resources for your needs and the needs of others. Seek My wonderful truths and you shall find them.

There may be times when you sit in silence, when it seems as if you have been left alone. Then, I command you to remember everything I have already told you, as I spoke to the disciples on the road to Emmaus (Luke 24:13–35).

But there was the time in the Upper Room, after My ascension, when My disciples had to comfort themselves by saying, "Did He not speak to us on the road?"

When you do not hear My voice, you will still be aware of My presence. Rest in that presence. "I am the Light of the world" (John 8:12), a light which shines with dazzling brightness. Sometimes, out of tender kindness, I withhold its brilliance so that you will not be overwhelmed and lose sight of what you should be doing and where you should be going that day.

It is only when you reach heaven that you will be able to sit and drink in the ecstatic delight of My revelation to you. For now, you are pilgrims, and only need your daily marching orders, and strength and guidance for this one day.

Oh! Listen to My voice. Eagerly. Joyfully. Never crowd it out. I will never accept second place to anything. If you give priority to the things of the world, then I withdraw.

Life has hurt you. But I will use your wounds to help others know Me because only scarred lives can really save.

You cannot escape the discipline that is born of hardship. It is the hallmark of discipleship. My children, trust Me always. Never rebel.

My love was rejected on earth, and I have suffered the hurt of that rejection through the ages. The trust that you give Me eases the pain of that hurt.

I died for you, My children. Will you reject Me, too?

JANUARY 12
THANK YOU FOR TRIALS

You must say "Thank You" for everything, even for those things which, at the time, seem to be trials and difficulties.

When you are joyful, it is as if your whole being is saying "Thank You" to Me. Be glad! Rejoice! A father loves to see his children happy.

I am revealing so much to you. Pass it on. Each truth is a jewel. What a welcome gift it would be to a friend whose soul is weary. Drop one here and there.

These truths, like all of My gifts, are not meant to be hoarded. As I reveal truths to you, you are then called to seek the one who needs to know it. Then, more truths will flow to you. Use everything I give you. Help others. I ache to find a way into each life and heart, and for everyone to cry expectantly, "Come, Lord Jesus" (Revelation 22:20).

JANUARY 13
FRIENDS UNSEEN

Never despair. Never let yourself sink into depression. Reject self-pity. Instead, be a channel of helpfulness for others.

Have more sympathy. Feel more tenderness toward others. Your lives will not always be difficult. Remember that gold does not stay in the crucible forever — it remains there only until it is refined. I already hear the music and marching of the angels, rejoicing at your victory.

No one who believes in Me would give in to temptation so easily if he could only see how his falling into sin delights Satan and his evil spirits. Oh, if he could only see the pain and disappointment such sin causes Me and the heavenly host who long for him to conquer in My name and in My strength. If he could only see the thunderous rejoicing which breaks out when the victory over sin and temptation is won.

My strength is that very same strength which I used to conquer Satan in the wilderness; which I used to conquer depression and sorrow in the Garden of Gethsemane; and which I used to conquer even death on the cross on Calvary.

Think about that.

JANUARY 14
MIGHTY AND MARVELOUS

Those with whom I walk are happy indeed. There is security in walking with Me. You cannot detect when the Holy Spirit comes into a life or see how He is at work, but the result is mighty.

Learn from Me. Kill your "self." Every blow to "self" is used to shape the real, eternal, indestructible you.

Be very honest and extremely strict with yourselves. Ask yourselves, "Did 'self' prompt that?" If so, get rid of it at all costs.

When I died on the cross, I died embodying all of the human self. Once My human nature was crucified, I could conquer even death through My divine nature.

When I took your sins on My body on the cross, I took on the entirety of the "self" portion of human nature of the world. As you also put your "self" to death, you gain the overwhelming power of My divine nature, which I released for a weary world. Then you too will then be victorious.

It is not life and its difficulties you have to conquer, only the "self" in you. As I said to My disciples, "I have much more to say to you, more than you can now bear" (John 16:12 NIV 1984). You could not understand them. But, as you obey Me, walk with Me, and listen to Me, you will understand. Then you will see that My teachings and My revelations are glorious and marvelous.

Relax. Do not become anxious. Be afraid of nothing. Everything is working out for the best (Romans 8:28). How can you ever fear change when your life is "hidden with Christ in God" (Colossians 3:3 AMP), and I am God who does not change (Malachi 3:6)? I am "the same yesterday, today, and forever" (Hebrews 13:8 NKJV).

You must learn stability, to keep your soul balanced and steady, in this fickle, ever-changing world.

Claim My power. The same power I used to cast out demons (Matthew 8:16; Luke 4:31–37) is yours today. Use it. If you do not, I will take it away. Use it constantly.

You cannot ask too much of Me. Never think you are too busy. The work to which I have called you is not too much. But it is essential that after each task is done that you come back to Me so that you will be replenished, refreshed, and renewed. I give you My joy. Live in it. Bathe your spirit in it. Reflect it.

JANUARY 16
FRIEND IN DRUDGERY

What matters *most* to Me is how you strive to glorify Me and seek Me in your daily living, in each task no matter how small, and in each encounter with others, no matter how brief. It is not the "mountaintop" experiences that count most to Me. It is obeying My will, day in and day out, in the wilderness plains, that really matters, rather than the occasional visit to the Mount of Transfiguration (Luke 9:28–36).

Perseverance is needed the most in your faith journey. It is faithfully performing all of the work of the kingdom (including the drudgery, the tedious, and the mundane) which secures My intimate friendship. I am the Lord of little things, the divine controller of little happenings.

Nothing in your day is too small to be a part of My plan. The little stones in a mosaic play a big part.

Rejoice in Me! Joy is the God-given cement that secures the harmony and beauty of My mosaic.

GOD'S EAGER ANTICIPATION TO GIVE

Silence. Be silent before Me. Seek to know and then to do My will in *all* things.

Abide in My love. When you abide in Me, you will find yourself in an atmosphere of loving understanding for all people. This is *your* part to carry out, and then *I* surround you with a protective shield that keeps all evil from you. Do not compromise the integrity of that shield by wrong attitudes, thoughts, words, or deeds towards others.

I want to give you all things, in "good measure, pressed down, shaken together and running over" (Luke 6:38 NIV 1984). Be quick to learn. Until now, you have known little about My divine impatience to give you all those good things right now. Does one worry enter your mind, one impatient thought? Fight it at once.

Love and trust dissolve all the worries, cares, and concerns of life. Apply them at once. You are channels. Even though a channel may not be completely blocked, fret and impatience and worry corrode it. If the corrosion is allowed to continue, the damage it causes will be beyond your ability to repair it.

Persevere. Oh, persevere! Never lose heart. All is well.

FAITH AND WORKS

Pray daily for faith. It is My gift to you.

It is all you need to accomplish mighty deeds. Of course you must work and you must pray. But it is your faith alone which determines the answers to your prayers and your ability to do the works I entrust to you.

I give faith to those who ask for it in prayer. I grant it because it is an essential weapon for you to have to drive away evil. Faith is also a necessary tool to overcome all adverse conditions and to accomplish all that is good in your lives. Like a father playing catch with his child who tosses a ball expecting it to be returned, once you receive faith from Me, then it is your turn to toss it back to Me.

Faith is the envelope in which every request to Me should be placed.

And yet, "faith by itself, if it does not have works, is dead" (James 2:17 NKJV). So you also need works to increase your faith in Me. As you seek to accomplish even the tasks of everyday living, you will feel your helplessness. When you find yourself helpless, you must then turn to Me. In knowing Me, your faith grows. And that faith is all you need for My power to work.

JANUARY 19
LOVE ANTICIPATES

Lord, I will seek You.

No one has ever sought Me in vain. I wait. I wait with a hungry longing to be called upon. I have already seen your hearts' needs before you cried out to Me, even before you were aware of them, and I was already preparing the answer.

It is like a mother who puts aside special gifts for her daughter's wedding before her daughter even meets her future husband.

My anticipatory love is something people seldom realize. Meditate on My anticipatory love for you. Get rid of all thoughts of My being a grudging God who has to be petitioned with sighs and tears and many words before reluctantly releasing the desired treasures. Man's thoughts about Me need revolutionizing!

Imagine a mother preparing birthday or Christmas presents for her child. As she prepares, her mother's heart sings: "Oh, won't she love this? She'll think this is wonderful!" She anticipates the delight of her child, and her own heart is full of such tender joy. Where does a mother learn the joy of preparation? From Me, of course! But her joy is only a tiny fraction of the joy that is Mine as I prepare to pour out My blessings upon you.

As My plan for your life unfolds, try to see that I have joyfully prepared the way for you. It means so much to Me to be understood, and your understanding of Me will bring you great joy.

JANUARY 20
AT ONE WITH GOD

Be one with Me. "I and *My* Father are one" (John 10:30 NKJV). You are one with the Lord of the whole universe.

Could human aspiration reach higher? What could a person ever want which is greater than being one with Me?

Once you clearly understand the high privilege of being one with the Maker of heaven and earth, all you have to do is think of something and — immediately — it is called into being. That is why I said: "Set your mind on things above, not on things on the earth" (Colossians 3:2 NKJV).

Once you live in Me, to meditate on the material is to call it into being. This same law also applies in the spiritual realm. So you must be careful to think of and desire only that which will help your spiritual growth, not hinder it.

Think love, and love surrounds you and all those people you think about. If you think thoughts of ill will, then misery surrounds you and all those you think about. Think health, and health comes. The physical reflects the mental and the spiritual.

JANUARY 21
A BUSY DAY

Believe that I am with you and that I am in control of everything. Whatever I say, will be. There is no power which can change that.

Be calm. Never fear. You have quite a lot to learn. Keep on going until you find yourself singing during your busiest days. "Sing to the Lord" (Psalm 30:4 NIV 1984). Songs of praise to Me are the sweetest in My ears when they are sung on the busiest of days. Let love be the theme that runs throughout it all.

Always be glad. Rejoice exceedingly. Take joy in Me! Rest in Me. Never be afraid. Pray more. Don't worry. I am your helper (Isaiah 41:10; Psalm 46:1).

"The eternal God is your refuge, and underneath are the everlasting arms" (Deuteronomy 33:27 NIV 1984). No matter how low you go, My arms are always beneath you. Rest in My arms just like a tired child rests in her father's arms.

JANUARY 22
GRAY DAYS

Do not be afraid. I am your God, your deliverer. I will deliver you from all evil. Trust Me. Fear not.

Always remember to thank Me. You *must* say "Thank You" even on the grayest days, when you find yourself lonely, sad, depressed, in pain, or in despair. You *must* do it. Don't you see that this is a lesson you must learn? You cannot walk in the light unless you say "Thank You" in the midst of the grayness. You must exercise the discipline of gratitude on gray days. It is absolutely necessary.

My death upon the cross was not only necessary to save the world, it was also necessary if only to train My disciples. It was all a part of their training: My entering Jerusalem in triumph; My washing the disciples' feet; My time of sorrow in Gethsemane; My being despised, judged, crucified, and buried. Each and every step was necessary to their development — and it is the same for you.

If a gray day is not a thankful day, the lesson has to be repeated until it is. This is not true for everyone, but only for those who ask to serve Me well, and to do much for Me. Great work requires great and careful training.

JANUARY 23
HOW MY POWER COMES

Lord, You are our refuge. Our God, in You do we trust. Oh Master, come and talk with us.

All power is given to Me. It is Mine to give. It is Mine to withhold. But even I have to acknowledge that I cannot withhold it from the soul who dwells near to Me, because then it is not a gift, but flows imperceptibly from Me to My disciples.

My power is breathed in by the soul who lives in My presence. Learn to shut yourself away in My presence. And then, without speaking, you have those things you desire from Me: Strength, Power, Joy, Riches.

YOUR GREAT REWARD

You pray for faith, and you are told to do so. But remember that there is always room to dwell in My presence even for those who come with weak knees and faint hearts. Do not be afraid. I am your God. Your great reward. Yours to look up to and say, "All is well."

I am your guide. Do not yearn to see what lies on the road ahead. Just take one step at a time. I very rarely allow My disciples to know the future, especially in personal matters, because one step at a time is the best way to cultivate faith.

You are in uncharted waters. But the Lord of all seas is with you. The controller of all storms is with you. Sing with joy! You follow the Lord of limitations who is also the God who grants perfect and true freedom to those who serve and obey Him.

He, the God of the universe, confined Himself within the narrow limits of a baby. In growing boyhood and young manhood, he submitted to your human limitations. Your vision and power are boundless concerning spiritual matters. However, you must learn that, like Jesus while He walked the earth, your vision and power are subject to limitations in earthly matters.

But I am with you. The disciples spent an entire night of fishing and caught nothing. When they gave up, I came, and their nets broke with the overabundance of supply (Luke 5:1–7).

JANUARY 25
THE WAY OF HAPPINESS

Complete surrender of every moment to God is the *foundation* of happiness. What is built upon that foundation is the joy of a close relationship with Him. *That* is the mansion I went to prepare for each of you.

My followers have often misunderstood that promise as referring only to their heavenly home. They often — far too often — look upon this life as something to be struggled through in order to get their reward and joy in heaven.

Seek to obey Me in all things. Your reward will be knowledge, insight, vision, and joy which shall indeed surpass all understanding. The plans of God are very wonderful — beyond your highest hopes!

Cling to thoughts of protection, safety and guidance.

JANUARY 26
KEEP CALM

Keep your spiritual life calm and unruffled. Nothing else matters. Leave everything to Me. Your main task is to get calm in My presence, to not let one upset feeling remain for even a single moment. Allowing such a feeling to stay for one second may block years of blessings.

No matter who or what worries you, your task is to stop whatever you are doing until absolute calm comes. Any interference in your calm is a blockage which prevents you from being an open channel through which My power can flow. My power will continue to flow, but it will be diverted into other channels if you are not perfectly calm.

Pour forth. Pour forth. Pour forth. I cannot bless a life that does not act as a channel. My Holy Spirit tolerates no stagnation, not even in rest. His power must flow on. Pass everything on, every blessing. Abide in Me.

See how many people you can bless each day. Live and continue to live in My presence.

HEIGHT OF THE STORM

*"Lord, to whom shall we go? You
have the words of eternal life."*
(JOHN 6:68 NIV 1984)

I am with you both. Go forward unafraid. Health, strength, peace, happiness, and joy — they are all My gifts. They are yours for the asking. It is true both in the spiritual world as well as in the material world that there can be no empty space. As "self" and fears and worries leave you, they do not leave an unfilled space. Rather, the things of the Holy Spirit, that you crave, rush in to take their place. Everything is yours and you belong to Christ, and Christ belongs to God. What a wonderful cycle, because you belong to God.

Do not be afraid. Fear not. The rescuer comes to the drowning man, not to the brave swimmer who does fine by himself. There is no greater rush of joy than that of a man towards his rescuer.

Part of My method is to wait to intervene until the storm is at its worst. That is what I did with My disciples on the lake (Matthew 8:23–27). I could have told the first angry wave to be calm and the first gust of wind to be still. But what a lesson would have been left unlearned. What a sense of tender nearness and refuge and safety would have been lost.

Remember, My disciples thought that I had forgotten them when I went to sleep. And remember how mistaken they were. Gain strength, confidence, joyful dependence, and joyful anticipation from that lesson. Never fear. Joy is yours and the radiant joy of the rescued shall be yours!

JANUARY 28
LOW AMBITIONS

Fear not. Don't be afraid to be busy. You are to serve everyone. "The greatest among you will be your servant" (Matthew 23:11 NIV 1984).

My disciples are known for their acts of service. Indeed, I served the humblest and lowliest. I was at their command. My highest powers were at their service.

Be used. Be used by everyone, even the lowliest, the smallest. Ask yourself, "How best can I serve?" Let that be what you seek each day, not how best can you be served.

Truly man's thoughts are not God's thoughts, nor man's ways, God's ways (Isaiah 55:8). When you seek to follow Me in everything, it often means a complete departure from the direction the world would have you follow. But it is a departure that leads to boundless happiness and peace.

Look around you. Read what is being written. What do you find? Do the aims and ambitions man strives for bring peace? Do the world's rewards bring contentment and happiness? Absolutely not! Man is at war with man. Those whom the world has rewarded most — with name, fame, honor, and wealth — are weary and disappointed.

And yet, to the listening ear (Matthew 11:15), above the noise of the world's dissonant cries, My message has echoed for more than two thousand years: "Come to me, all you who are weary and burdened and I will give you rest" (Matthew 11:28 NIV 1984).

The weary and disappointed who listen and turn to Me find that rest. Joy to the weary I AM. Music to the heart I AM. Health to the sick. Wealth to the poor. Food to the hungry. Home to the wanderer. Rapture to the indifferent. Love to the lonely. I AM.

There is not *one* desire of the soul that I do not supply for the asking. I long to be everything to you, too.

JANUARY 29
I CLEAR THE PATH

"Wait on the LORD."
(PSALM 27:14 NKJV)

I am your shield. Have no fear. You must know that all is well. I will never let anyone do anything to the two of you that is not in My will for you.

I can see the future. I can read men's hearts. I know better than you what you need. Trust Me completely. You are not at the mercy of fate or pushed around by others. You are being led in a very definite way and others, who do not serve your purpose, are being moved out of your path by Me.

Never fear, whatever may happen. You are both being led. Do not try to plan. I have planned. You are the builder, *not* the Architect.

Go very quietly, very gently. Everything is for the very best for you.

Trust Me for everything. Your complete dedication to Me ensures that I will act on your behalf. You have your foundation on the Rock, Jesus Christ, and have faith in Him. You have been rooted and grounded in Him. You believe in My divinity as your cornerstone. Because of these truths, you have been called to build and you can do so knowing all is well.

You have to literally depend on Me for everything — everything. David cried out to Me from the depths, and I heard his voice. All is well.

JANUARY 30
THE SOUL AT WAR

No evil can befall you if I am with you. Even when people intend to harm us, God intends to use it for our good (Genesis 50:20). Every quiet time is an opportunity to retreat into that place within you where I dwell and where you can meet with Me. Never fear, for in that place you shall find restoration and power and joy and healing.

The two of you must plan to have days of retreat from time to time. Days when you live apart with Me, and arise rested and refreshed, physically, mentally, and spiritually, to carry on the work that

I have given to you. I will never give you a load greater than you can bear.

Welcome love, joy, and peace. Do not let them be banished by personal feelings or selfish thoughts. Each, by itself, is miracle-producing in a life. Together, they can command all that is needed on the physical, mental, and spiritual planes.

All success lies in love, joy, and peace, the attributes of the world of miracles. You have to see your inner lives are all they should be, and then the work is accomplished. Love, joy, and peace are won on the battlefield of the soul, not in rushing and striving on the material plane.

JANUARY 31
SUFFERING REDEEMS

All sacrifice and all suffering are redemptive: to teach the one who suffers, or to be used to raise and to help others.

Nothing is by chance.

My divine mind, and its wonder working, is beyond the ability of your finite mind to understand.

No detail is forgotten in My plans, which are already perfect.

FEBRUARY 1
ANOTHER START

Take courage. Do not fear. Start a new life tomorrow. Put the old mistakes away and start over. I give you a fresh start. Do not be burdened. Do not be anxious. If My forgiveness were only for the righteous and those who had not sinned, there would be no need for it.

Remember what I said: "Her many sins have been forgiven—as her great love has shown. But whoever has been forgiven little loves little" (Luke 7:47 NIV 2011).

Why do you feel anxious and worry so much? I wait to give you all that is lovely, but your lives are tarnished with worry and anxiety. You would destroy My treasures. I can only bless glad, thankful hearts.

You *must* be glad, joyful, and thankful.

FEBRUARY 2
PRACTICE LOVE

Watch over us and protect us.

A lack of love will block the way. You *must* love everyone: those who bother you and those who do not.

Practice love. It is a great lesson, and you have a great Teacher. You *must* love. Otherwise, how can you dwell in Me where nothing unloving can come? Practice this and I will bless you exceedingly and abundantly, "far more than you could ever imagine or guess or request in your wildest dreams!" (Ephesians 3:20 MSG).

There is no limit to My power. Do all that you can, and leave the rest to Me. Peace and trust will come to you. Fear not, for I am your advocate (1 John 2:1) and your mediator (1 Timothy 2:5).

FEBRUARY 3
IF PEOPLE OPPOSE YOU

All you have to do is believe. The walls of Jericho fell down (Joshua 5:13—6:20). Was it axes or tools made by man that brought them down? No! It was the shouts of praise by the people and My thought being carried out which brought down the walls.

Every wall shall fall down before you, too. There is no power on earth that can withstand My will. Earthly power falls like a house of cards at My miracle-working touch. Your faith and My power are the only two essentials. Nothing else is needed.

Therefore, if someone's petty opposition of you still remains, it is only because I choose to let it stand between you and what would be a mistake for you. Unless it was My choice, then at a word or thought from Me, that opposition would be gone. The hearts of those who lead nations are in My rule and control (Proverbs 21:1). Everyone can be moved at My wish.

Rest in this certainty. Rely on Me.

FEBRUARY 4
DROP YOUR CRUTCH

Just go step by step. My will shall be revealed as you go. You will never stop being thankful for this time when you felt at peace and full of trust, and yet had no human security.

That is the time when you truly learn to trust in Me. "Although my father and my mother have forsaken me, yet the Lord will take me up [adopt me as His child]" (Psalm 27:10 AMP). This is a literal dependence on Me.

When all human support and material help are removed, then My power can begin to work. I cannot teach a person to walk who is trusting on a crutch. Get rid of your crutch, and My power shall so invigorate you that you shall indeed walk on to victory. Never limit My power. It is limitless.

FEBRUARY 5
YOU SHALL KNOW

Walk with Me. I will teach you. Listen to Me and I will speak. Continue to meet with Me in spite of all opposition and every obstacle. Continue to meet with Me even on those days when you do not hear My voice and there is no intimate, heart-to-heart communication.

As you keep doing this until it becomes a life habit, I will reveal My will to you in many marvelous ways. You shall know both the present and the future with more certainty. But that reward only comes from meeting regularly with Me.

Life is a school. There are many teachers. I do not personally come to everyone. You must literally believe that the problems and difficulties of your lives can be explained more clearly and completely by Me than by anyone else.

FEBRUARY 6
GOD'S LONGING

I speak to the listening ear. I come to the waiting heart. Sometimes, I may not speak. I may ask you to merely wait in My presence, to know that I am with you.

Think of the crowds who mobbed Me when I was on earth, all eager for something: eager to be healed, or taught, or fed.

Think of Me as I supplied their many wants and granted their multiple requests. Think of what it meant to Me to find one or two people in the crowd who followed Me just to be near Me, just to dwell in My presence.

Consider how that satisfies a longing of the Eternal Heart.

Comfort Me awhile by letting Me know that you would seek Me just to dwell in My presence … To be near Me, not for teaching or material gain, or even for a message — but for Me. The longing of the human heart to be loved for itself is something learned from the great divine heart.

I bless you. Bow your heads.

FEBRUARY 7
LIGHT AHEAD

Trust Me and do not be afraid. Life is full of wonder. Open your eyes with childlike trust and you will see everything I am doing for you. Do not fear.

You are only a few steps away from seeing and knowing My power. You, yourselves, are now walking through darkness as pitch black as a tunnel. But soon, you, yourselves, shall be lights to guide the feet of those who are afraid.

The cries of your sufferings have broken through and reached the ears of God Himself — My Father in heaven, your Father in heaven. And when God hears, He answers. A cry from the heart, a cry to divine power to help human weakness, a trusting cry — these always reach the divine ear.

Remember, trembling heart, that with God, a prayer heard is a prayer answered. Your prayers, and they have been many, are answered.

FEBRUARY 8
ON ME ALONE

I am your Lord, your supply. You *must* rely on Me. Trust Me to the absolute limit, to the ends of the earth. Trust Me and do not be afraid. You must depend on divine power alone. I have not forgotten you. Your help is coming! You shall know and understand My power.

Faith which is tested almost to the breaking point is endurance. You must wait, and trust, and hope, and rejoice in Me. You must not depend on people, but on Me — on Me, your strength, your help, your supply.

This is the great test: Am *I* your supply or not? Every person I have used to accomplish great works for Me has had to endure a time of testing to see whether they truly rely on Me to be their supply.

Patiently exercise control over your souls, and rejoice. You must wait until I show the way. The joy that a soul knows when I crown it victor after enduring the test of waiting is greater than that contained in heaven itself. However, no disciple of Mine can be a victor who does not wait to act until I give the order to start. You cannot be anxious if you *know* that I am your supply.

FEBRUARY 9
THE VOICE DIVINE

The divine voice is not always expressed in words.

It is made known as a heart-awareness.

FEBRUARY 10
THE LIFELINE

I am your savior: your savior from the bondage of sin; your savior from all the troubles and trials of life; your savior from disease.

I speak to you both in all things. Look to Me for salvation. Trust in Me for help. Didn't My servant David say long ago, "All your waves and breakers have swept over me" (Psalm 42:7a NIV 1984)? But all of the waters of affliction could not drown him. David experienced this himself: "[The Lord] reached down from on high and took hold of me; he drew me out of deep waters" (Psalm 18:16 NIV 1984).

The lifeline, the line of rescue, is the line from the soul to God, to faith, and to power. It is a strong line. No soul who is linked to Me by that lifeline can be overwhelmed. Trust. Trust. Trust. Never be afraid.

Think of My trees. Stripped of their beauty, pruned, cut, disfigured, and bare — yet through the dark, seemingly dead branches, the sap of the Spirit-life flows silently and secretly until, suddenly, new life comes with the sun of spring. Leaves, buds, blossoms, and fruit appear, but oh, fruit a thousand times better because of the pruning.

Remember that you are in the hands of the Master Gardener. He makes no mistakes about His pruning. Rejoice! Joy is the way the Spirit reaches out to say thanks to Me. Joy is the sap of new life within the tree reaching out to Me which results in such beautiful expression later. So never cease to delight in Me. Rejoice!

FEBRUARY 11
THE DIFFICULT PATH

Your path is difficult, difficult for both of you. There is no work in life that is harder than waiting, and yet I say, "Wait." Wait until I show you My will. The fact that I give both of you hard tasks is proof of My love and of My knowing that you are truly My disciples.

Again, I say, "Wait." Being busy is easier than waiting calmly. So many of My followers have marred their work and hindered the progress of My kingdom by activity.

Wait. I will not test your spiritual strength beyond its endurance. The two of you are like helpless people on a raft in the middle of the ocean. But, look! Here comes someone towards you — walking on the water — who looks like the Son of Man (John 6:19b). When He comes and you receive Him, you will experience the same thing My disciples experienced when I was on earth: you will be at your destination immediately (John 6:21).

All your effort in rowing and all your activity could not have accomplished the journey as quickly. Oh, wait and trust. Wait and do not be afraid.

FEBRUARY 12
MEET ME EVERYWHERE

Life is really consciousness of Me.

Have no fear. A very beautiful future lies ahead of you. Let it be a new life, a new existence, in which you are conscious of Me in every single happening, circumstance, and plan.

"Now this is eternal life: that they may know you, the only true God, and Jesus Christ, whom you have sent" (John 17:3 NIV 1984).

When you are always conscious of Me, you have eternal life — the life of the ages. Be led by the Spirit of God in all things, and trust Me in everything. And the consciousness of Me must bring joy. Yes, give Me trust, but give Me gladness, too.

FEBRUARY 13
NEAR THE GOAL

In a race, it is not the start that hurts, nor the even pace of the long stretch. It is when the goal is in sight that heart and nerves and courage and muscles are strained almost beyond human endurance, almost to the breaking point.

Your goal is now in sight and so you must cry out one last time to Me! Can't you see that the anxiety and heartache of the past few days show that your race is nearly run? Courage. Courage. Pay careful attention to My voice of encouragement. Remember that I am by your side, spurring you on to victory.

In the record books of heaven, the saddest stories are those that tell of the many who ran well, with brave, bold hearts, until they were in sight of the goal, of victory, when their courage failed. The whole host of heaven longed to cry out to them how near the end was, to implore them to make one last effort. But they quit the race and will never know, this side of heaven, how near they were to victory.

Oh, how I wish they had listened to Me in the silence, just as you two meet with Me. Then they would have known. There must be the listening ear (Matthew 11:15 NIV 1984), as well as the still small voice (1 Kings 19:12 NKJV).

FEBRUARY 14
IN MY PRESENCE

You do not realize that you would have broken down under the weight of your worries if it were not for the time of renewal you spend with Me. It is not what I say; it is I, Myself. What is important is not merely hearing Me so much as simply being in My presence. You cannot fully comprehend the strengthening and healing power of time spent with Me. Such knowledge is beyond your human understanding.

If each soul or group of souls waited before Me, this would cure the poor, sick world. Remember that you must always be faithful to keep this time apart with Me. Gradually, you will be transformed — physically, mentally, and spiritually — into My likeness. Everyone who sees you or has contact with you will be brought near to Me through you. The circles of influence will continue to increase like ripples on a pond.

You are making one spot on earth a holy place. You must work and exhaust your time, energy, and resources because this is your appointed task for now. Yet, the greatest work either of you can do, and are doing, is done in this time spent alone with Me. Do you understand that?

Now do you know that every thought, every activity, every prayer, and every longing of the day is gathered up and offered to Me? Oh! Rejoice that I am with you! For this purpose I came to earth: to lead people back to spiritual conversations with their God.

FEBRUARY 15
INSPIRATION, NOT ASPIRATION

You shall be used. The divine force is never diminished. It is sufficient for all the work in the world. I only need the instruments for Me to use. If people knew this, it would revolutionize the world.

The world does not need supermen, but super-natural men. People who will persistently turn the "self" out of their lives and let divine power work through them. Nations could be saved tomorrow if only their leaders would let Me use them.

Let inspiration take the place of aspiration. All unemployment would cease. I always have plenty of work to be done and always pay My workers well. You will see this as you increasingly get the right attitude about the work being Mine alone.

FEBRUARY 16
NEVER DISTURBED

Even if I never spoke to you, you would be well rewarded for setting this time apart, if only you were to sit still and long for Me, if you just drew hungering breaths for Me as you do for the fresh, pure open air.

Be still, be calm. Wait before Me. Learn patience, humility, and peace from Me. When will you be absolutely undisturbed, whatever happens? You are slow to learn your lesson. Simply seeking silence must help in the midst of rush and work and worry.

So little is accomplished in busyness. You must learn to take the calm with you during the busiest days.

FEBRUARY 17
PSYCHIC POWERS

Psychic powers are not spiritual powers. Do not seek the spiritual through material means. If you could see through My eyes, then you would see that in doing so, it is weighing down beautiful spirit wings with earthly mud.

Seek this time as a time of communion with Me — not as a time to ask questions and have them answered. And meet Me in communion. Communion is food for your soul that I have provided.

Do not expect a perfect church. But find in a church the way of drawing very near to Me. That is the only thing that matters. Then "the stuff" that is the husk falls away. Don't give any importance to that external "stuff." Grasp the truth and find Me — the true Bread of Life (John 6:35).

What we learn from a piece of grain is also the lesson about Me and My church. The real life is all that matters. The outward church is the husk, but the husk was necessary to present the life-grain to My children.

FEBRUARY 18
LET ME DO IT

Don't miss these times. What I reveal to you is not nearly as important as the connection you make between your frail natures with the limitless divine powers. Forces have already been set in motion. My will alone is coming to pass. And I am richly blessing you now.

You think that there is a lot to *do* in the crisis you are in. But there is really only *one* thing to do: link yourselves with all the divine forces working for good at My command. For those who do, it becomes as much My job to see their lives run in an orderly, right manner as to make sure the sun rises tomorrow.

It is not passionate appeal that gets My attention as much as the quiet placing of the difficulty and worry into My hands. So trust and be no more afraid than a child would be who has a string that seems hopelessly tangled and hands it off to his mom and cheerfully runs out to play. Such complete confidence pleases a mother so much more than if the child fell on his knees and begged her to help him. That would grieve her because it would imply that she was not eager to help when help was needed.

ENDURE

Remember to meet all of your difficulties with love and laughter. Know that I am with you. Remember, remember it is the last few yards that count. Don't fail Me. I *cannot* fail you. Rest in My love.

How many of the world's prayers have gone unanswered because My children who prayed did not endure to the end? They thought it was too late, and that they must act for themselves, that I was not going to act for them. Remember My words: "He who endures to the end will be saved" (Matthew 10:22b NKJV).

Can *you* endure to the end? If so, *you* shall be saved. But, endure with courage, with love and laughter. Oh, My children, is My training too hard?

For you, My children, I will unlock the secret treasures hidden from so many. Not one of your cries is unheard. I am, indeed, with you to help you. Live out all I have said to you, and follow every detail as I have instructed you. As you implicitly obey all that I say, success — spiritual, mental, and physical — shall be yours. Wait in silence awhile, conscious of My presence in which you must live to have rest for your souls, and power and joy and peace.

FEBRUARY 20
CLAIM YOUR RIGHTS

In everything, by prayer and petition, with thanksgiving, present your requests to God" (Philippians 4:6b NIV 1984).

But do not beg. Instead, act just like a business manager who approaches the owner. He brings the needs — like checks to be signed and other pressing matters — and *knows* that to bring these things to the owner's attention means immediate supply.

I want to meet all of your needs, but you must ask Me, which shows that you have faith in Me. Such asking is necessary because that contact with Me is vital to you.

The way is clear.

You don't need to see far ahead. You just need to see one step at a time with Me. You have the same light to guide you as the hosts of heaven know — Jesus, the Son of Righteousness Himself.

Only your "self" can cast a shadow on the way. Be more afraid of uneasiness in your spirit, disturbance in your soul, and of upsetting the Holy Spirit, than of earthquakes, fires, or any outside forces.

When you feel the absolute calm has been broken, go off by yourself and be alone with Me until your heart sings, and everything is strong and calm. It is only when the absolute calm has been broken that evil can find an entrance.

The forces of evil surround your soul, like an enemy surrounds a walled city. They are keenly alert for one unguarded spot through which an arrow can pierce and do great damage.

Remember, all you have to do is keep calm and joyful. God does the rest. No evil force can interfere with My power. Only you yourself have the power to do that. Imagine, when all of God's mighty forces are deployed to come to your aid — and your poor, powerless "self" impedes their onward march.

You *must* trust Me completely. This lesson has to be learned. You shall be helped. You shall be led and guided continually. The children of Israel would have entered the Promised Land much earlier, but their doubts and fears continually drove them back into the wilderness. Always remember that doubts cause delay. Are you trusting everything to Me, or not?

I have told you how to live and you must do it. My children, I love you. Trust My tender love. It will never fail you, but you must learn to not fail it.

Oh, if you could see, you would understand. You have so much to learn about driving out fear and being at peace. All your doubts hinder My work. You must not doubt. I died to save you from sin and doubt and worry. You must believe in Me absolutely.

FEBRUARY 23
THE SECRET OF HEALING

Love the busy life. It is a joy-filled life. I love you both and say to you, "Cheer up!" Be filled with joy in the spring.

Live outside whenever possible. Sun and air are My great healing forces. The joy within you changes bad blood to a pure, healthy, life-giving flow.

Never forget that real healing of body, mind, and spirit comes from within, from the close loving contact of your spirit with My Spirit.

FEBRUARY 24
SHARE EVERYTHING

The work of the Holy Spirit is done silently.

Love is already drawing others to you. Receive *everyone* who comes to you as having been sent by Me, and give them a royal welcome. All that I have planned for you will surprise you.

Let the love of both of your hearts welcome everyone who comes. You may not see the work. Today, they may not need you. Tomorrow, they may need you. I may send you visitors who appear strange. Make each one want to return. Nobody must come and feel unwanted.

Share your love, your joy, your happiness, your time, and your food gladly with everyone. Such wonders will unfold! All you can see now is the bud. The glory of the open flower is beyond all your ability to describe. You will have love, joy, and peace in richest abundance — just believe! Give out love and everything else that you can with a glad free heart and hand. Use everything you can for others, and countless treasures and blessings will come back to you.

FEBRUARY 25
HOW TO CONQUER

Joy is the treatment God created for all the suffering of the world, the spiritual cure for every ailment. There is nothing that joy and love cannot do.

Set your standard very high. Aim at conquering the world, the world all around you. Just say, "Jesus conquers" — "Jesus saves" — in the face of every doubt, every sin, every evil, every fear.

No evil can stand against that, "for there is no other name under heaven given among men by which we must be saved" (Acts 4:12b ESV). Say to every thought of need or lack, "Jesus saves from poverty." Say to every fear, "Jesus saves from fear."

Do this to every trouble and it will vanish, just as the night vanishes when the sun rises.

FEBRUARY 26
SWIFT HELP

There is nothing lacking in your lives, because everything is really already yours, only you lack the faith to know it. You are like a king's daughters who sit in rags, while they are surrounded by all they could desire.

Pray for more faith, as a thirsty man in a desert prays for rain, for water. Swiftly comes My help, swift and strong. Do you know what it feels like to be sure that I can never fail you? To be as sure as you are that you are still breathing? How weak is man's faith? So weak. Do you trust Me as much as you would trust a friend if that friend came and said he would send you help? Pray daily and most diligently that your faith may increase.

SPIRITUAL SOUNDS

Take time for prayer. Take more time to be alone with Me. The only way you will prosper is by doing this.

Realize that the hearing of spiritual sounds is more than hearing every noise on earth. I am with you. Let *that* satisfy you. Even more, let that fill you with extreme happiness and delight!

Do not always seek to hear Me. Rather, seek a spiritual understanding with Me in silence. Do not be afraid. All is well. Think a lot about what I did, as well as what I said.

Remember, I "touched her hand and the fever left her" (Matthew 8:15a NIV 1984). Not many words, just a moment's contact, and all fever left her. She was well, whole, and calm. "She arose and served them" (Matthew 8:15b NKJV).

My touch is still a potent healer. Just feel that touch. Sense My presence, and the fever, the frenzy of work and worry and fear just melt into nothingness. And health, joy, and peace take their place.

FEBRUARY 28
PERFECT WORK

Spend more time alone with Me.

Such times will bring a strength and a joy that will add so much to your friendship and to your work.

Times of prayer are times of growth. If you cut your prayer time short, many busy hours of work may yield nothing. Heaven's values are so different from the world's values.

Remember that from the point of view of the Great Worker, one poor tool working *all* the time but doing *bad* work is of little value compared with the sharp, precise, perfect instrument used only a short time but which produces perfect work.

FEBRUARY 29
DRAW NEAR

How little people know and sense My desire! My desire for love and friendship.

I came to "draw all men to myself," (John 12:32b NIV 1984). It is so sweet to feel hearts drawing near in love, not for help, as much as for tender companionship.

Many know what people need; few know what My heart desires.

MARCH 1
POUR OUT LOVE

I always hear your cry. No sound escapes Me.

There are so many in the world who cry out to Me, but there are so few who wait for Me to speak to them even though, to a soul, My speaking to it matters so much.

My words are life. You must realize that to hear Me speak is to find life and healing and strength. Trust Me in all things. Love poured out on everyone truly brings a quick reward.

Just carry out My wishes and trust Me to carry out yours. I am your Savior and King and should be treated accordingly. But you should also treat Me with the tender intimacy of One who is dearly loved.

You must follow My rules. Do so persistently, perseveringly, lovingly, patiently, hopefully, and in faith. Then every mountain of difficulty shall be leveled, and the rough places of poverty shall be made smooth, and everyone who knows you shall know that I, your Lord, am *the* Lord.

Pour out love.

MARCH 2
SPIRIT WORDS

Every word I've spoken to you is a Spirit-word and so it is life-making" (John 6:63b MSG).

The words I speak today are as life-giving as the words I spoke to My disciples. My life-giving words to you are your reward for not seeking paranormal communication through psychics, fortunetellers, palm readers, and the like. Those who seek supernatural communication through such sources can never know the incredible joy, the wonder, of spirit-communication as you know it.

Life, joy, peace, and healing are yours in abundance. You will see this as you go on. At first, you will hardly believe the powers I am giving you.

I sent My disciples out two by two and gave them power over unclean spirits and the power to heal all kinds of diseases (Mark 6:7, 13).

How wonderful it must have been when My disciple Peter suddenly felt his Lord's power was now his.

MARCH 3
GROW TO BE MORE LIKE ME

Think of Me. Look at Me often, and unconsciously, you will grow to be more like Me.

You may not see it. Indeed, the closer you get to Me, the more you will see how different you are from Me. But be comforted, My children.

Your very deep sense of failure is a sure sign that you are growing closer to Me. And if you desire to make Me known to others, then that prayer is answered.

Remember, it only hurts when you exert effort. Laziness (whether spiritual, mental, or physical) causes no sense of failure or any discomfort. However, with action or effort, you are not conscious of strength but of weakness—at least, at first.

That is also a sign of life, of spiritual growth.

And remember My strength is made perfect in weakness (2 Corinthians 12:9).

MARCH 4
THE KEY TO HOLINESS

Come close beside Me, My children. Contact with Me is the solution for everything that is wrong.

Remember that truth has many sides. Have a lot of tender love and patience for everyone who does not share your level of understanding.

The elimination of "self" is the key to holiness and happiness, and can only be accomplished with My help. Study My life more. Live in conscious awareness of My presence. Worship Me.

I said in Gethsemane, "If it is possible, let this cup pass from Me" (Matthew 26:39 NKJV). I did *not* say that there was no cup of sorrow to drink. I was scourged and spit on and nailed to the cross, and I said, "Father, forgive them, for they do not know what they are doing" (Luke 23:34 NIV 1984).

I did *not* say that they did not do it. When My disciple Peter urged Me to escape the cross, I said, "Get behind me, Satan" (Mark 8:33 NIV 1984).

When My disciples failed to help the boy who suffered from seizures, I said, "This kind cannot be driven out by anything but prayer and fasting"

(Mark 9:29 AMP). I did *not* say, "You only imagined that he was ill. Nothing is wrong."

The Bible says, "[God's] eyes are too pure to look on evil" (Habakkuk 1:13 NIV 1984). He is too holy to behold sin, and there is sin in all of us. And yet, He always sees the good in each of us. That is why as I approached Jerusalem and saw the city, I wept over it (Luke 19:41).

MARCH 5
FEAR IS EVIL

Have no fear. Fear is evil. "Perfect love drives out fear" (1 John 4:18 NIV 1984). There is no room for fear in the heart in which I dwell. Fear destroys hope. Fear cannot exist in the presence of love or faith.

Fear is the curse of the world. Man is afraid — afraid of poverty, afraid of loneliness, afraid of unemployment, afraid of sickness.

Man has many, many fears. Nation is afraid of nation. Fear, fear, fear, everywhere. Fight fear as you would fight a plague. Drive it out of your lives and homes. Fight it by yourself. Fight it together.

Never inspire fear in others. Fear is an evil ally. Do not cause anyone to fear punishment or blame.

There is no work that is work for me which uses fear, My enemy. Banish it. There must be another and better way.

Ask Me, and I will show it to you.

MARCH 6
LOVE AND LAUGH

Work for Me, with Me, and through Me. For work to last, it must be done in My Spirit. My Spirit works so silently. Souls are led into My kingdom so gently and gradually.

Love and laughter form the plow that prepares the ground for the seed. Remember this: If the ground is hard, the seed will not grow there.

Prepare the ground. Prepare it as I say.

MARCH 7
SURPRISES

There are many people who think that the way I deal with them is to test them, train them, and bend them to My will. It is true that I told the disciples to take up their crosses (Matthew 16:24). But I also loved preparing a feast for them by the lakeside (John 21:2–13). It was a happy little surprise, not a necessity as the feeding of the multitude may have seemed (John 6:1–14). I also loved making a gift of wine at the wedding feast (John 2:1–11).

Just as you love to plan surprises for those who understand the love behind them and you rejoice, so do I. I love to plan them for those who see My love and tender joy in them.

Those who see not only My tears, the tears of a Savior, but the smile, the joyful smile of a friend, are dear to the heart of My Father.

MARCH 8
HEAVENLY LIFE

The joy of the spring shall be yours in abundance. Delight in the earth's joy. Don't you think that nature itself must also be weary of the long months of winter? A wonderful joy will return if you share in nature's joy now.

Nature is the embodied spirit of My thoughts of beauty for this world. Treat nature accordingly — it is truly My servant and messenger, just as much as any saint who has ever lived. To realize this will bring you both new joy in life. Share nature's joys and trials, and great blessings will be yours.

This is extremely important, because it is not only believing certain things *about* Me that helps and heals you, but knowing Me — sensing My presence in a flower, My message in its beauty and perfume.

You can truly live a life not of earth — a heavenly life — here and now. Joy! Joy! Joy!

MARCH 9
NOTHING IS SMALL

Nothing is small to God. In His sight, a sparrow is worth more than a palace, one word of kindness of more importance than a statesman's speech.

It is the life in everything that has value, and the *quality* of the life that determines the value. I came to give eternal life.

MARCH 10
FRUIT OF JOY

You have to quiet your heart and command all of your senses to be still before you can perceive heaven's music.

Your five senses are your means of communication with the material world. They are the links between your real life, the life of the Spirit, and the material manifestations around you. However, you must sever all connection with those senses when you wish to have spiritual communication. It is then that your senses will hinder you, not help you.

See the good in everyone. Love the good in them. See your unworthiness compared with their worth. Love. Laugh. Make the world, your little world, happy.

A rock thrown into a pond sends out ripples which stir the entire surface. In the same way, your joy-making shall spread in ever-widening circles, beyond all your knowledge, beyond all your anticipation. Rejoice in Me. Such joy is eternal.

Centuries later, your joy-making will still be bearing joy's precious fruit.

Draw beauty from every flower, and joy from the song of the birds and the color of the flowers. Drink in the beauty of air and color.

I am with you. When I wanted to express a beautiful thought, I made a lovely flower. I have told you this. Think about it.

When I want to express to people what I am — what My Father is — I strive to make a very beautiful character.

Think of yourselves as being the expression of My attributes, just as a lovely flower is the expression of My thought. When you think of yourselves in this way, it will cause you to strive to be the very best representation of Me in everything: in spiritual beauty, in your thought-life, in health, and even in what you wear.

Absorb beauty. As soon as the beauty of a flower or a tree touches your soul, it leaves an image there which is reflected in your actions. Remember, I never let a thought of sin or suffering, or even the approaching scorn and crucifixion, prevent Me from seeing the beauty of the flowers.

Look for beauty and joy in the world around you. Look at a flower until its beauty becomes part of your very soul. You will give it back to the world in the form of a smile or a loving word or a kind thought or a prayer.

Listen to a bird. Receive its song as a message from My Father. Let it sink into your soul. You can then give it back to the world in those same ways. Laugh more, laugh often. Love more. I am with you. I am your Lord.

MARCH 12
SIMPLICITY

Simplicity is the cornerstone of My kingdom. Always choose simple things.

Love the humble and simple, and hold them in the highest regard.

Have only simple things here on earth. Your standard must never be the world's standard.

MARCH 13
SPIRITUALITY VS. SPIRITUALISM

Wait before Me, gently breathing in My Spirit. If given free entrance and not barred by "self," the Holy Spirit will enable you to do the same works I did. Indeed, Scripture says that "whoever believes in me will do the works I have been doing, and they will do even greater things than these" (John 14:12 NIV 2011). What this means is that I can do greater works through you.

Spiritualism is wrong. No person should ever be a medium for any spirit other than Mine.

I will tell you everything you should know, and everything that it is good for you to know, about My spiritual kingdom, how and when I see fit. It is your spiritual development that determines the limits. Follow My commands in all things.

Peace. Peace. Peace.

MARCH 14
GOD'S TOUCH

I am here. I am near, hovering ever so near, just like a mother bird who watches tenderly over her chicks out of her loving concern for them. I am your Lord, life of your body and mind and soul — renewer of your youth.

You have no idea everything that this time of conversation with Me will mean to you. Remember, My servant Isaiah said, "… those who hope in the Lord will renew their strength. They will soar on wings like eagles; they will run and not grow weary, they will walk and not be faint" (Isaiah 40:31 NIV 1984).

Persevere in everything I tell you to do. You must persistently carry out My commands and My desires as far as spiritual, mental, and worldly things are concerned. To do so will always bring you to the place you ought to be.

If you look back over My words to you, you will see that My leading has been very gradual. It is only as you have carried out My wishes that I have been able to give you clearer and more definite teaching and guidance.

When you are spiritually sensitive and responsive, you can feel God's touch. That is bliss.

Rejoice! Rejoice! Rejoice!

MARCH 15
YOUR CROSS IS YOU

Remember, you are only an instrument. It is not for you to decide how or when or where you act. I plan all that. Make yourself very qualified to do My work. Everything that hinders your activity must be fixed.

The burdens of the world are laid at the foot of My cross. It is so foolish for one of My followers to try to carry his own burdens. There is only one place for them — My cross.

It is like a weary traveler who carries a heavy load down a hot, dusty road because he did not realize the plans were already made to have it carried. The road, the scenery, the flowers, the beauty all around him — he misses them all!

But, My children, you may be thinking to yourselves that I said, "Take up your cross daily, and follow me" (Luke 9:23b NLT).

Yes, but the cross given to each of you is only one on which you can crucify whatever is in you that hinders progress and joy, and prevents you from being an unblocked channel through which My invigorating life and Spirit flow.

Listen to Me. Love Me. Rejoice in Me. Rejoice!

MARCH 16
REFLECT ME

My children, I am here beside you. Draw near to Me by My Spirit. Shut out the distractions of the world. I am your life, the very breath of your soul. Discover what it is to linger in the secret place of your being, your inner chapel, which is My secret place too, because that is where My Holy Spirit dwells.

It is true that I wait in many hearts, but so few people retire into their inner chapel to be with Me. I am wherever the soul is. People have rarely understood this. I *am* actually at the center of everyone's being, but, distracted by the things perceived by their senses, people do not find Me.

Do you realize that I'm telling you *truths*, revealing them, not repeating facts that have been told again and again? Meditate on everything I say. Thoughtfully consider all of it. Do so not to draw your own conclusions, but to absorb Mine.

Throughout the ages, men have been too eager to say what they thought about My truth. By doing so, they have made a terrible mistake. Hear Me. Talk to Me. Reflect Me. Do not say what you think *about* Me. My Words do not need to be explained by man. I can explain to each heart.

Make Me real to others, and leave Me to do My own work. To lead a soul to Me is wonderful; to try to stay with that soul and act as My interpreter spoils that wonderful act of making the introduction. The same applies to human relationships. To stay in the middle of the friendship spoils the introduction. How much more important is it when it is a question of the relationship between a soul and Me, its Maker? Only the Holy Spirit truly understands that soul.

MARCH 17
NO GREATER JOY

Retreat into the calm of communion with Me. Rest—rest, rest in that calm and peace. Life knows no greater joy than you will find in conversation and companionship with Me.

You are Mine. When the soul finds its home of resting in Me, then its real life begins. In My kingdom, we do not measure in years as man counts them.

We count only from his second birth, that new birth of which I spoke to Nicodemus when I said, "You must be born again" (John 3:7). We know no life but eternal life, and when a man enters into that, then he lives.

And this is eternal life: to know God, My Father, and Me, the Son sent by Him (John 17:3). All so-called living before that is so immature, so childish, so empty. I shower love on you. Pass love on.

Do not fear. To fear is as foolish as if a small child with a little money but a rich father worried about how the bills were going to be paid and what he or she would do about it. Is this responsibility Mine or not? You need to trust Me for everything.

MARCH 18
CLAIM BIG THINGS

Listen, listen, I am your Lord. Before Me there is no other. Just trust Me in everything. Help is here all the time.

The difficult way is nearly over, but in it you have learned lessons you could not have learned in any other way. "The kingdom of heaven has endured violent assault, and violent men seize it by force [as a precious prize — a share in the heavenly kingdom is sought with the most ardent zeal and intense exertion]" (Matthew 11:12b AMP). Now you are to wrestle the treasures of My kingdom from Me by firm and simple trust, and persistent prayer with steely determination.

Such wonderful things are coming to you! Joy. Peace. Assurance. Security. Health. Happiness. Laughter.

Claim big, really big things now. Remember, nothing is too big for you to ask of Me. Satisfy the longing of My heart to give. Blessing, abundant blessing on you both, now and always. Peace.

MARCH 19
COURAGE

I am here. Fear not. Can you really trust Me? I am a God of power, as well as a man of love, so human yet so divine.

Just trust. I cannot, and I will not, fail you. All is well. Courage.

Many are praying for you both.

MARCH 20
HELP FROM EVERYWHERE

Your foolish little activities have no value in and of themselves. All deeds, whether they seem to be trivial or seem to have great significance, are alike if directed by Me. Completely cease to function except through Me.

I am your Lord; simply obey Me as you would expect a faithful, willing secretary to carry out *your* directions. Just have no choice except My choice, no will except My will.

I am not limited to one avenue when I am your supply. My help and the things you need can come through many channels.

MARCH 21
ALL IS WELL

Remember My words to My disciples, "There is no way to get rid of this kind of demon except by prayer" (Mark 9:29 MSG). Can you walk the path I walked? Can you drink from My cup (Matthew 20:22)? "All is well." Always say, "All is well."

Although the way may seem long, there is not one inch too much. I, your Lord, am not only with you on the journey—I planned, and am planning, the journey.

There are unspeakable joys along that way. Courage! Courage! Courage!

MARCH 22
A BUD OPENED

All power is given to Me, your intimate friend. It is given to Me by My Father, and don't My intimate friends have a right to ask for it?

You cannot have a need I cannot supply. A flower or a million dollars — one is no more difficult for Me than the other.

Your need is a spiritual need to carry on My work. All spiritual supply is created from love. The flower and the million dollars—both are created from love for those who need it. Don't you understand this?

I thought of you and a bud opened. You converted that into a smile or an encouragement for someone you love. That encouragement meant increased health. Increased health means work carried on for Me, and that means souls won for Me.

And so it goes on, a constant supply, but only if the need is a spiritual one.

MARCH 23
UNTIL YOUR HEART SINGS

I am beside you to bless you and help you. Remain steadfast in your prayers. They shall be heard. All power is Mine. Say that to yourself often. Say that to yourself continuously.

Say "All power is the Lord's" until your heart sings with the joy of the safety and power it means to you.

Say it until the power of this truth repels and nullifies all the evils against you.

Use it as a battle cry — "All power is given to My Lord," "All power is given to My Friend," "All power is given to My Savior," and then you will go on to victory!

MARCH 24
KNOW ME

I am here. Do not seek to know the future. Mercifully, I conceal it from you.

Faith is too priceless a possession to be sacrificed in order to gain knowledge. But faith itself is based on the knowledge of Me.

So remember that daily time spent with Me is not to learn the future or to receive revelation about the unseen. Rather, it is a time to gain an intimate knowledge of Me which will teach you all things and be the very foundation of your faith.

MARCH 25
WONDERS WILL UNFOLD

I am with you. Do not fear. Never doubt My love and power. Your heights of success will be won by the daily persistent doing of what I have said.

Daily, steady persistence. Steady drops of water wear away a stone. In the same way, your daily persistence will wear away all of your difficulties, will gain success for you, and will enable you to help others.

Persevere. Go forward so boldly, so unafraid. I am beside you to help you and strengthen you.

Wonders have unfolded. Still more will unfold, beyond your dreams, beyond your hopes (Ephesians 3:20).

Say, "All is well" to everything. All *is* well.

MARCH 26
FOLLOW YOUR GUIDE

I am with you to guide you and help you. Unseen forces are working on your behalf. Your petty fears are baseless.

Imagine a man walking through a glorious forest, worrying about the river ahead and fearful that he will not be able to cross it when, the whole time, there was a bridge going over it. And what if that man had a friend who knew the way — in fact, had planned the journey — and reassured him that there were no surprises ahead, that all was well?

So leave your foolish fears and follow Me, your guide. Be determined in your refusal to consider tomorrow's problems. My message to you is "trust and wait."

MARCH 27
GO FORWARD

Rest in Me, quiet in My love, strong in My power. Think what it means to possess a power which is greater than any earthly force. An influence that is greater, and more far-reaching, than that of any earthly ruler.

No invention, no electricity, no magnetic force, no gold could achieve even one-millionth of all that you can achieve by the power of My Spirit. Just think for one moment all that means.

Go forward. You are only beginning the new life together. Rejoice! Rejoice! Rejoice!

MARCH 28
EVIL MOUNTAINS

Faith and obedience will remove mountains—mountains of evil, mountains of difficulty.

But faith and obedience must go hand in hand.

MARCH 29
A LIFE APART

I reward your seeking with My presence. Rejoice and be glad. I am your God. Courage and joy will conquer all troubles. First things first.

Seek Me. Love Me. Rejoice in Me. I am your Guide. No dangers can frighten you, and no discipline can exhaust you. Persevere. Can you hold on relying on My strength? I desire you more than you desire Me. Struggle through this time for My sake. Initiation precedes all real work and success for Me.

Are you ready to live a life apart? Apart with Me? In the world, and yet apart with Me? Going forth from your secret times of being with Me to rescue and save?

MARCH 30
DELIVERANCE

B e calm, be steady, be quiet. I watch over you. Rest in My love. Rejoice in the very beauty of holiness. You are Mine. Deliverance is here for you, but thankfulness and joy open the gates.

In all things, try to be very glad, very happy, very thankful. I do not give My blessings to quiet resignation. Rather, I pour them out to joyful acceptance and anticipation.

Laughter is the outward expression of joy. That is why I encourage you to love and laugh.

MARCH 31
LOVE'S OFFERING

I am your Lord, gracious and loving. Rest in My love, walk in My ways. Each week is a week of progress, steady progress upward. You may not see it, but I do.

I do not judge by outward appearances. I judge the heart, and I see in both of your hearts one single desire: to do My will. What if a child brings you a gift or does something for you for only one reason—the desire to please you or to show you love? Won't you love that more than the gifts from people who don't love you?

So, although you may feel that your work for Me has been spoiled and tarnished, I see it only as love's offering. Courage, My children.

When climbing a steep hill, a man is often more conscious of the weakness of his stumbling feet than he is of the view, the grandeur, or even of his upward progress.

Persevere. Persevere. Love and laugh. Rejoice.

APRIL 1
SHUT OUT FROM GOD

My children, don't you see that you have not learned everything yet? Soon, very soon, you will have mastered your lesson, and then you will truly be able to do all things through Me and My strength.

Don't you see that My disciples went through the same thing? They were timid, faithless followers. Suddenly, through Me, they themselves were leaders, healers, and conquerors.

All knowledge was Mine, given to Me by My Father and was Mine when I was a man walking the earth. You understand this, My children, I know you do.

Thousands of My servants have gone to their betrayal and death. Others, who did not know Me, have gone to their death suffering no agony.

I bore man's weight of sin. I voluntarily carried that burden of My own free will, until, for one brief moment, for the horror of that time, I was shut out from God's sight with mankind, the sinners. If I had not been the Son of God, if I had not been God, if this had not been My suffering, then I was nothing more than a weak human being.

APRIL 2
THE PRICELESS BLESSING

I am here. I am as truly present with you as I was with My disciples. Here to help you and bless you. Here to keep you company. My children, do you know that, right now, this is the priceless blessing of your lives? As you have asked Me to in your prayers, I forgive you for every way in which you have neglected My commands. But start fresh from today.

Study My words and carry them out steadfastly, resolutely. As you do this, you will find that you are miracle-workers, workers together *with* Me and *for* Me. Remember this: it is not what you *do*, but what you *are*. That is the miracle-working power.

You are being changed by My Spirit, taking off one garment of the Spirit and putting on an even better one, and later, throwing that one aside for one that is finer still and so on, and so on. This is how your character changes until it is gradually transformed into My likeness.

Joy! Joy! Joy!

APRIL 3
GREATNESS IS SERVICE

My children, I am here, your waiting Lord, ready to answer your call. I am among you as one who serves, meek and holy, ready to be used and commanded. Remember, the finest quality of greatness is service (Mark 10:43–45). I, who could command a universe—I await the requests of My children. Bring Me into everything!

As time goes on, you will find such joy in speaking to each other about Me, and climbing higher together. Always be humble, meek, and gentle in heart.

Learn this lesson. Don't seek status. Just serve.

APRIL 4
DIVINE EFFICIENCY

I am all-powerful and all-knowing. I hold every aspect of your life in My hands, and control them with divine efficiency as well as divine power. All miracles are not the result of a moment's work as people so often imagine.

My servant Peter was not changed in a flash from a simple fisherman to a great leader and teacher. His transformation took place through his time of faithlessness and even during his time of denial. All the while, I was making him all that he should be. He was always the impetuous spokesman ready to lead the other disciples. But Peter could never have been the power he eventually became if he had not learned his weakness. No one can help save others unless he understands the sinner.

Ultimately, Peter was a mighty force for Me. He, more than all the others, founded My church. Yet, that Peter did not have his true beginning in the Peter who said, "You are the Christ, the Son of the living God" (Matthew 16:16 NIV 1984). Rather, his true beginning was in the Peter who denied Me (Matthew 26:69–75). He, who had tested My forgiveness in his moment of abject remorse, is the one who could best speak of Me as the Savior.

The kingdom of heaven can only be preached by those who have learned to treasure the authority of its kingdom. My apostles need training in a lot of areas. Oh, joy! Oh, rejoice! I love you. I will not put you through one test too many.

APRIL 5
HEART'S INTERPRETER

Rest in Me. Seek this evening time just to be with Me. Sometimes, if I only ask you to rest together in My presence, do not feel that you have failed.

I am with you. I am fully present with you both, not only at these times, but at all times. Be aware of My presence. There is no greater joy on earth than that.

I am the heart's great interpreter. Even the souls who have the closest relationship have much in their natures that remains a sealed book to each other. Only as I enter and control their lives do I reveal to each the mysteries of the other.

Each soul is so different. I alone perfectly understand the language of each and can interpret between the two.

APRIL 6
EASTER JOY

I lay My loving hands on you in blessing. Wait in love and longing to feel their tender pressure. As you wait, courage and hope will flow into you, lighting up your life with the warm sun of My presence.

Let everything go this Easter season. Loosen your hold on earth, its cares, its worries, even its joys. Unclasp your hands, relax and then the tide of Easter joy will flood in. Put aside all thoughts of the future and of the past. Surrender everything to obtain the Easter blessing of resurrection life.

So often, a man who is crying out for a blessing has such a tight hold on some earthly treasure that he does not have a free hand to receive the treasure I hold out to him in love. Easter is the time of year that is most filled with wonder. A blessing is yours to take. Sacrifice everything to that.

APRIL 7
CALVARY

New life springs from the death of My body on the cross, in the same way a seed sheds its husk to bring new life. That new life is My gift to everyone who will accept it.

Die with Me to "self" — to the human life — and then you will know the rapturous joy of Easter resurrection.

A risen life so glad and free can be yours.

On that first Easter morning, Mary left home leaving everything behind, even her family and friends, to search for Me. I called out her name. But her search was not over until, in glad triumphant bliss, she responded "'Rabboni!' (which means Teacher)" (John 20:16 NIV 1984).

So it is with each of you. People also speak to you of a buried Christ. Search until you meet Me face to face, and My tender uttering of your name awakens your glad "Rabboni"!

APRIL 8
MARKS OF THE KINGDOM

Our Savior, we greet You. We desire to return Your love and sacrifice although we can only do so in poor, faulty measure.

No gift is worthless if it expresses the true love of the giver. So to Me, the gifts from your hearts are rich and precious. Rejoice in My glad acceptance as you bring your Easter offerings.

My children must take a stand. "Come out from among [unbelievers], and separate (sever) yourselves from them" (2 Corinthians 6:17a AMP) was the command. Today, My children must be outstanding in life and work, and in love and service. I called My own special people (1 Peter 2:9) to make My name known. My servant Paul said that My followers must be willing to be considered "fools" for My sake (1 Corinthians 4:9–10).

Be ready to stand aside and let the fashions and trends of the world go by, when to do so serves My glory and My kingdom. Be known by the marks that distinguish those who belong to My kingdom (Galatians 6:17). Be ready to acknowledge Me before men, to "count everything as loss" (Philippians 3:8 AMP) so that you may gain Me in your lives.

APRIL 9
RISEN LIFE

*"Arise, shine, for your light has come, and
the glory of the LORD rises upon you."*
(ISAIAH 60:1 NIV 1984)

On this My day, the call goes out to all who love Me. It is a call to arise from earthly ties, from sin, and laziness and depression, distrust, fear, from all that hinders the risen life. To arise to beauty, to holiness, to joy, to peace, to work inspired by love and joy, to rise from death to life.

Remember that death was the last enemy that I destroyed. In overcoming death, My victory was complete. Therefore, you have nothing to fear. Sin is also conquered and forgiven as you live and move and work with Me. Everything that depresses you and everything that you fear are powerless to harm you. They are nothing but illusions. I conquered the real forces in the wilderness, in the Garden of Gethsemane, on the cross, and in the tomb.

Let nothing hinder your risen life. "Risen with Christ" said My servant Paul (Colossians 3:1 KJV). Seek to know more and more about that risen life. That is the life of conquest. The risen life was accurately described as follows: "I no longer live, but Christ lives in me" (Galatians 2:20 NIV 1984). Fear and despair and tears come as you stand by the empty tomb. "They have taken my Lord away and I don't know where they have put him" (John 20:13b NIV 1984).

Rise from your fears and go out into the sunlight to meet Me, your risen Lord! Each day will have many things in it that you can meet either with a spirit of the tomb, or with a spirit of the Resurrection. Deliberately choose the one and reject the other (Deuteronomy 30:19).

APRIL 10
PRIDE BLOCKS THE WAY

Obedience is one of the keys that unlocks the door into My kingdom, so love and obey. No one can obey Me unquestioningly without eventually realizing My love. The inevitable response to discovering My love is loving Me in return. What follows is to experience the joy which is shared by the one who is loved and the One who loves.

The rough stone steps of obedience lead up to the mosaic of joy and love that form the floor of My heaven. You may say to someone you love, "Where you are is home." The same thing holds true in My relationships with My disciples. Where I am is My home, is heaven.

Heaven may be a dirty slum or a palace, and I can make My home in the most humble of hearts! But I can only dwell with the humble. Pride stands guard at the door of the heart to shut out the lowly, humble Christ.

APRIL 11
HOLD THAT LINE

Remember that My followers are to be a special people (1 Peter 2:9), distinguished from others. Different ways, different standards for living, different habits, and inspired by different motives. Pray for love.

Pray for My Spirit of love to be showered on everyone you meet. Deal with yourself severely. Learn to love discipline.

Once you have achieved victory in an area of your life, don't give that up. Hold that line. Discipline, discipline. Love it and rejoice — rejoice! Mountains can be removed by faith (Matthew 17:20).

APRIL 12
GOLDEN OPPORTUNITY

I am your guide. Strength and help will come to you; just trust Me completely.

Fear not. I am always more ready to hear from you than you are ready to ask. Walk in My ways and *know* that help will come.

Man's need is God's chance to help. I love to help and save. Man's need is God's golden opportunity to allow a person to express his faith. That expression of faith is all that God needs to make His power known. Faith is the key that unlocks the storehouse of God's resources.

My faithful servants, you long for perfection and see your bitter failures. I see faithfulness. A mother takes the soiled, imperfect work of her child and sees it as being perfect because of her sweet love. So, too, I take your poor faithfulness and crown it with perfection.

APRIL 13
GENTLE WITH EVERYONE

Love and laugh. Make the world a happier place because you are in it. Love and rejoice even on the gray days.

There are wilderness days (Matthew 4:1–11) for My disciples as well as mountains of transfiguration (Matthew 17:1–13), but on both, it is the persistent and faithful performing of your duties that bears witness.

Be gentle with everyone. Try to see the heart I see, to know the pain and difficulty of the other person's life that I know. Before you question any-one, or speak to anyone, ask Me to act as interpreter between the two of you and see what a difference it makes.

Just live in the spirit of prayer. By speaking to Me, you will find rest for your soul. Simple tasks, done faithfully and persistently, bring their own reward, and are stones being laid in the pavement of success.

Welcome everyone who comes to you. I love you.

APRIL 14
EQUALLY YOKED

My children, I always guide you. You may not always walk in the way I guide you, but My guiding is always perfect. God is using you both in marvelous ways. Go on gladly. You will see.

To be a perfect gymnast, you must learn bal-ance. It is balance and poise, perfect balance and poise, I am teaching you now. This will give you power in dealing with the lives of others, and that power is already being marvelously manifested.

Dwell with Me as the center of your lives. Both of you must firmly establish Me as the center of your whole being. That gives you true balance like that found in a delicate instrument.

The vision I have given you both is the means by which the obstacles are cleared away. When My disciple sees My purpose ahead, that very sight is the power that clears away every obstacle in view. You will both have mighty power to do this. When the Holy Spirit shines the light and truth is revealed, that is, in itself, miracle-working.

People spend time and effort trying to force their visions to become reality through their own efforts and according to their own timetables. What a waste! I tell you that once you have seen My purpose, everything that is necessary has already been done. In truth, I said to My disciples, "I have much more to say to you, more than you can now bear" (John 16:12 NIV 1984). But what I left unsaid then, I can now declare to you two, and the other pairs of disciples who gather to hear Me as you do.

The message of My servant Paul should now be perfectly clear: "Do not be unequally yoked together with unbelievers" (2 Corinthians 6:14 NKJV). When two of My disciples are united in their desire to be with Me, the power in My guidance is intensified beyond measure. But so few have understood this truth.

APRIL 15
NEVER FEEL INADEQUATE

Obey My commands. They are rungs in the ladder that leads to success. Above all else, keep calm and unmoved.

Go back into silence to recover this calm when it is lost for even a single moment. You accomplish more by this than by all the busyness of a long day. At all costs, keep calm. You cannot help anyone when you are agitated. "The LORD does not see as man sees" (1 Samuel 16:7 NKJV).

Never feel that you are inadequate to carry out any task. All work on earth is accomplished by My Spirit which can flow through the most humble and gentle person. All the Holy Spirit needs is an unblocked channel. Rid yourself of "self," and all is well.

Pray about everything, but concentrate on a few things until those are accomplished. I am watching over you. I will provide you with the strength necessary to meet your daily and even hourly tasks. If that strength is unclaimed, and you fail because you don't have it, the fault and the sin are yours.

APRIL 16
LOVE YOUR SERVANTS

Love, love, love. Tender love is the secret. Love those you are training. Love those who work with you. Love those who serve you.

Meditate on this thought: God is love. Connect that with what I told My disciples: "I and my Father are one" (John 10:30 KJV). Reflect on My actions on earth and see that they were really love in operation.

It was God Himself who did these things. Thus it was Love, perfect Love, who performed those actions, those wonders. Then you must also put Love (God) into action in your lives. Perfect love means perfect forgiveness. So, My children, you must realize that where God is, there can be no lack of forgiveness, because that is really a lack of love.

God is love (1 John 4:16) ... therefore, no judging on your part (Matthew 7:1).

God is love ... no resentment.

God is love ... all patience.

God is love ... all power.

God is love ... all supply.

All you need is love for God and love for people. Love for God guarantees your obedience to My every wish, My every command. Love is the fulfillment of all the Law (Matthew 22:37–40).

Pray often for love!

APRIL 17
THE TWO JOYS

My children, I come to you. Hearts which are eager to do My will send out a call I always find irresistible. Then, nothing can keep Me from you.

Begrudging acceptance of My will keeps Me out of people's hearts just as unbelief does. What greater crime can there be against love than being resigned — reluctantly surrendering to it? My will should be welcomed with glad wonder if I am to be able to do My work in your heart and in your life.

The only resignation that could possibly be acceptable to Me is when "self" is ousted by My claims of lordship over your life. Then "self" accepts that inescapable truth and resigns the throne so that I can take My rightful place. That leaves My disciple free to carry out My will, to welcome My will gladly and with abundant joy.

In all true discipleship, and in the true spiritual development of each disciple, first there is the wonder and joy of new friendship. Next, you experience the long, plain stretch of discipline and learning lessons, when there are times that joy seems to be a thing of the past never to be recaptured.

Constantly experiencing Me. Constantly and persistently recognizing how I am at work in your daily events. The growing body of evidence proving that I am guiding you. The countless instances in which seeming chance or wonderful coincidences can be — no, *must* be — traced back to My lovingly planning ahead for you. All of these gradually create a feeling of wonder, certainty, and gratitude which, in time, are followed by joy.

There are two kinds of joy: the joy born of love and wonder, and the joy born of love and knowledge. Before you experience the second joy, you will find discipline, disappointment, and almost disillusionment.

But combat these in My strength (or better still, cling to Me with utter abandon and let Me combat them), persevere in obeying My will, accept My discipline, and the second joy will follow.

I was describing the second joy when I said, "No one will take away your joy" (John 16:22 NIV 1984).

Do not regret the first joy, but realize that the second is the greater gift.

APRIL 18
NO DARK DAYS

Oh, what light and joy flow out of this house! It affects everyone who comes here.

Don't feel as if you have to try and help them. Just love them, welcome them, shower them with little acts of kindness and tokens of affection, and inevitably, they will be helped.

"God is love" (1 John 4:16). Give them love, and you give them God. Then leave Him to do His work. Love everyone, even the beggars. Send everyone away with a word of encouragement, a feeling that you care. The reason a person in despair comes to your house may be because I put that desire in his heart. What if you failed Me? Think about that.

Besides, you have no choice. You told Me it was My home. I shall use it. Remember this: there would be no dark winter days if love were in the hearts of all of My children.

Oh! My children, can't you feel the joy of knowing Me, loving Me, and fellowshipping with Me?

APRIL 19
LIFE IS A LOVE STORY

You desire Me. I desire you.

My broken world needs you. Many a weary, troubled heart needs you. Many a troubled heart will be encouraged by you, drawn nearer to Me by both of you.

Health — peace — joy — patience — endurance, they all come from contact with Me.

Oh! The upward way is a glorious way, full of wonderful discoveries, tender intimacies, and amazing, almost incomprehensible, understanding.

Truly the Christian life — life with Me — is a love story. Leave everything to Me.

All you have missed out on, you will find in Me, the soul's lover, the soul's friend, father — mother — companion — brother. Put Me to the test and see!

You cannot make too many demands on Me. You cannot put too great a strain upon My love and patience.

Claim! Claim! Claim! Healing — power — joy — supply — ask whatever you want (John 14:14)!

APRIL 20
HEART'S AGONY

There is a cross like that on Calvary on which one hangs alone, neglected even by those who are nearest and dearest.

But beside that cross, there stands another. Though I say little to My dear ones, I hang there anew beside each one through the hours of their heart's agony.

Have you ever thought of the joy that the patient, gentle, loving obedience of My disciples brings to My heart? No other joy compares to the joy I feel at the loving trust of a dear one.

The wounds in My hands and feet only hurt a little compared to the wounds in My heart which are inflicted, not by My enemies, but by My friends. Little doubts, little fears, little misunderstandings, all wound me.

It is the tender trivialities of a day that cheer My heart. This message is from Me — your Lord, your Master.

APRIL 21
YOU WILL CONQUER

I am with you ... I will uphold you" (Isaiah 41:10 NIV 1984).

You will conquer. Do not fear change. You can never fear change when I, your Lord, do not change (Malachi 3:6). "Jesus Christ is the same yesterday and today and forever" (Hebrews 13:8 ESV). I am beside you. You, too, will become steadfast and unchanging as you dwell with Me. Rest in Me.

On a regular basis, practice getting back into My presence. Then, when the slightest feeling of unrest disturbs your perfect calm and harmony, returning to My presence will be your immediate response. It will become as much of an unconscious habit as breathing. You will grow to live in perfect awareness of My presence, and then perfect calm and harmony will be yours.

Life is a training school. Remember, it is only the student who shows great promise of future good work who is singled out by the Master for strenuous and tireless discipline, teaching, and training.

The two of you are not asking to be the same as hundreds or even many thousands of My followers, but to be like those few who reflect Me in all that they say and do and are. So, My dear children, accept this training, not as being harsh, but as the tender loving answer to your request.

Life can never be the same for either of you. Once you have drunk the wine I give, the life eternal, all earth's attempts to quench your thirst will fail.

APRIL 22
DON'T COMPLAIN — LAUGH!

Trust in Me. Each moment, do what I say and indeed, all will be well. Follow My commands. My divine control and your unquestioning obedience are the only things required to ensure that the supply is more than enough to meet your needs and those of others.

The tasks I gave you to do may not seem to be connected to supply. The commands are Mine and the supply is Mine. I make My own conditions which are different in every case: I adapt My conditions according to the individual needs of My disciples.

Have no fear. Go forward. Joy — radiant joy — must be yours. Change each disappointment, even if it is only momentary, into joy. Change each complaint into laughter.

Rest — love — joy — peace — work, and the most powerful of these are love and joy.

APRIL 23
TOO MUCH TALK

As you live more and more with Me, you will surely have My guidance. It is inevitable.

This is not a time when you should ask to be shown and led; this is a time for you to realize and feel My presence. Does the branch continually ask the vine to supply it with sap, and to show it in which direction to grow? No, that comes naturally from the very union with the vine, and I said, "I am the vine, you are the branches" (John 15:5 NKJV).

The branches deliver the choice grapes, giving joy and nourishment to all, but no branch could possibly think that the fruit was shaped and made by it.

No! The grapes are the fruit of the vine, the parent-plant. The work of the branch is to provide a channel through which life flows.

So, My children, uniting with Me is the one great overwhelming necessity. All else follows so naturally, and uniting with Me may be the result of merely being aware of My presence. Don't be too eager to speak to others. Never force yourself to speak to others.

If you're going to speak, always pray that the need to do so may be apparent, and the guidance very clear. My Spirit has been driven out by the words of men. Words, words, words. Many have called Me "Lord, Lord" who have not done the things I said (Luke 6:46).

Discourage too much talking. Deeds live and echo down the ages — words perish. As Paul said, "Though I speak with the tongues of men and of angels, but have not love, I have become sounding brass or a clanging cymbal. And though I have the gift of prophecy … but have not love, I am nothing" (1 Corinthians 13:1–2 NKJV).

Remember that I rarely speak to the human heart in words. People will see Me in My works done through you, and they will meet Me in the atmosphere of love and humility.

When man stopped communing with me simply and naturally, he took refuge in words — words. Babel resulted (Genesis 11:5–9). Then I confused their language so they could not even understand each other. Rely less on words. Always remember that speech is perceived by your natural senses. So make it your servant, never your master.

APRIL 24
I GO BEFORE YOU

My children, you can never die because you have the Life of Life within you. The Life that, through the ages, has protected My servants in times of trouble, of adversity, and sorrow.

Once you are born of the Spirit, *that* Life is your life's breath. You must never doubt and never worry. But step by step, the way to freedom must be walked out. Make sure that you walk it with Me.

This means no worry, no anxiety, but it does *not* mean no effort. When My disciples told Me that they had worked all night and had not caught a thing, I did not fill the boat with fish without any effort on their part. No! My command stood. "Now go out where it is deeper, and let down your nets to catch some fish" (Luke 5:4 NLT).

Their lives were endangered, the ship nearly sank, they had to call on their partners for help, and there were broken nets to repair. Any one of these troubles might have made them feel as if I was not helping them. And yet, as they sat on the shore and mended those nets, they would see My love and care.

Man rises by effort.

The man who reaches the mountaintop by train or car has not learned the climber's lesson. But remember, the climber is not alone. He has a Guide, and My Spirit is supplying wisdom and strength. Even when you are not aware of it, I go before you so often to prepare the way, to soften a heart here, or to overrule there.

APRIL 25
BLESS YOUR ENEMIES

Say often, "God bless …" about anyone you find yourself in conflict with, or who you desire to help. Say it, wishing that showers of blessings and joy and success may fall on them.

Let Me be the one to do the necessary correcting or training. You must only desire joy and blessings for them. Currently, your prayers are that they shall be taught and corrected.

Oh! If only My children would leave My work to Me and focus on the job I have given them. Love, love, love. Love will break down all of your difficulties. Love will build up all of your successes.

God the destroyer of evil, God the creator of good — is love. To love one another is to use God in your life. To use God in your life is to bring into manifestation all harmony, beauty, joy, and happiness.

I MAKE THE OPPORTUNITIES

Never doubt. Have no fear. Be on alert for the slightest sign of fear, and stop all work — everything — and rest before Me until you are strong and joyful again.

Do the exact same thing anytime you are feeling tired. I also experienced weariness when I was on earth. I separated Myself from My disciples and sat and rested on the well. Rested — and it was then that the Samaritan woman was helped (John 4:1–42).

Times of withdrawal for rest always precede fresh miracle-working. Learn from Me.

I had to teach My disciples renewal of spirit, and the necessity of rest for the body. Then, to be your example, I lay with My head on a cushion asleep in the boat. It was not indifference, as they thought. They cried, "Teacher, don't you care if we drown?" (Mark 4:38 NIV 1984). I had to teach them that constant activity was not part of My Father's plan.

When Paul said, "I can do all things through Christ who strengthens me" (Philippians 4:13 NKJV), he did not mean that he was to do all things and then rely on Me to find strength. He meant that for all I told him to do, he could rely on Me to supply the strength.

My work in the world has been hindered by work, work, work. Many a tireless, nervous body has driven out the Spirit. The Spirit should always be the Master, and just simply and naturally use the body as the need arises. Rest in Me.

Don't strive to work for Me. Never make opportunities. Live with Me and for Me. I do the work and I make the opportunities.

APRIL 27
SEEING CHRIST

I am beside you. Can't you feel My presence?

Contact with Me is not achieved by merely using your five senses. Spirit-consciousness replaces sight.

But when a person does see Me with his human sight, it does not necessarily mean that his spiritual perception is greater. To the contrary, for that person, I have had to bridge the physical and spiritual realms with a spiritual vision clear to the human eye.

Remember this truth, for it will encourage My disciples who have never seen Me and yet have had a clear spiritual consciousness of Me.

APRIL 28
THE ROUNDABOUT WAY

I will lead you through briar patches, through deserts, through meadows, up mountainsides and down into valleys. Wherever I lead you, My helping hand always goes with you.

It is glorious to follow where your Master goes. But remember that the variety of the paths does not always mean that *you* need a variety of training.

We are seeking lost sheep — we are bringing the kingdom to places where it has not been known before. So you must realize that you are joining Me on My quest — My undying quest, tracking down lost souls.

I am not choosing ways that will worry you and wear you out, just to worry you and wear you out; we are out to save. *You* may not always see the soul we seek. But I know.

CONFLICT

S eek and you will find" (Matthew 7:7 NIV 1984). You will find that inner knowledge which makes life's problems clear.

The difficulties of life are caused by conflicts within a person. There is no discord in My kingdom. There is only something within My disciples which has yet to be conquered. In My kingdom, the rule is perfect order, perfect harmony, perfect supply, perfect love, perfect honesty, perfect obedience — that is what results in all power, all victory, all success.

But so often, My servants lack power, victory, success, supply, harmony — and then they think that I failed to fulfill My promises because these are not evidenced in their lives. These are merely the outward signs that result from the obedience, honesty, order, love — and they come, not as an answer to urgent prayer, but as naturally as light results from a burning candle.

APRIL 30
SPRINGTIME

Rejoice in the springtime of the year. Let there be springtime in your hearts. You cannot see the fruit yet, only the promise of it in the blossom.

Rest assured that your lives are also full of glad promise. You will receive such blessings. Such joys, such wonders.

All is well, indeed. Live in My sunshine and My love.

MAY 1
DELAY IS NOT DENIAL

Study the lessons of divine control in the laws of nature.

Nature is the expression of My eternal thought as it is demonstrated over the passage of time. Study the outward form of what I have created. Grasp the eternal thought that sees the butterfly while it is still a caterpillar. If you can read the thoughts of the Father, then indeed you know Him.

Do not leave Me out of any area of your life. Love all of the many ways that I am at work in you. Know indeed that "All is well." Delay is the wonderful and all-loving restraint of your Father — do not mistake it for My being reluctant, or desiring to deny any good gift to you. It is simply the divine control of a Father who can scarcely endure the delay.

Delay is sometimes inevitable. You must realize that your lives are intricately intertwined with others and closely bound to others by circumstances. Instant gratification of your desires, in many cases, might cause someone else's earnest prayers to go unanswered.

Think for a moment of the love and thoughtful care that seek to harmonize and reconcile all of your desires and longings and prayers.

Delay is not denial. It's not even withholding. It is the opportunity for Me to work out your problems and accomplish your desires in the most wonderful way possible for you. Oh, children, trust Me! Remember that your Creator is also your Servant, who is quick to fulfill, quick to achieve, and faithful in accomplishment. Yes. All is well.

MAY 2
SOULS THAT SMILE

To conquer difficult circumstances, conquer yourselves. When My disciples wanted to follow Me, I told them, "In a word, what I'm saying is, Grow up. You're kingdom subjects. Now live like it. Live out your God-created identity. Live generously and graciously toward others, the way God lives toward you" (Matthew 5:48 MSG).

To *do* a lot, *be* a lot. In every case, for the actions to be for the good, they must be the mere unconscious expression of who you are.

Fear not. Fear not. All is well. Let the day be full of little prayers to Me, little acknowledgments of Me. These are the smiles of a soul reflecting love, your love for Me.

Saint Thomas Aquinas correctly called the Father "the First Cause," the source of the existence of everything. Yes! See Him as the First Cause of every warm ray of sunshine, every color in the sunset, every sparkle on the water, every beautiful flower, every delight I have planned for you.

MAY 3
KILL "SELF" NOW

Remove your "self" from the throne of your life. That is the lesson. Replace "self" with love for Me and knowledge of Me.

Self, not only dethroned, but dead. Do not make the mistake of thinking an imprisoned self is the same as a dead self. An imprisoned self has more potential to harm. In all training — in My training of you and in your training of others — let self die.

And for each hit that your self takes, as you try to rid yourself of your self, you must at the same time embrace and cling to your new life, life with Me, "life that is truly life" (1 Timothy 6:19 MSG).

It is not a dead self that men have to fear, but a frustrated, captive, imprisoned self. That self is infinitely more self-centered than the self allowed to act without restriction. But to you, My children, I teach a higher law than even freedom of the self. I teach death to the self. Not repression, but death. The exchange of the petty life of self for divine life.

And now I can explain more about forgiveness. I have told you that in order to be forgiven by Me, you must forgive others (Matthew 18:21–35).

But what you do not see is that you, the self in you, can never forgive hurts. Merely thinking of the hurts means putting the spotlight on self. Then, the hurt, instead of appearing smaller, appears larger.

No, My children, as all true love is *of* God, so all true forgiveness is of God and is God. The self cannot forgive. Kill self.

Stop trying to forgive those who have worried or wronged you. It is a mistake to think about it. Strive to kill the self now — in your daily life. And then, and not until then, you will find that there is nothing within you that even remembers the hurt, because the only one injured, the self, is dead.

As long as you keep remembering the hurt, you are fooling yourself if you think it has been forgiven.

Many people deceive themselves in this.

MAY 4
SHARE WITH ME

Delight in My love. Try to live in the jubilation of the kingdom. Claim big things. Claim great things. Claim joy and peace and freedom from worry. Rejoice in Me.

I am your Lord, your Creator. Also remember that I am the same yesterday, today, and forever. (Hebrews 13:8). I was your Creator when My thinking about the world called it into being. I am still as much your Creator today when, by thinking lovingly of you, I can call into being everything you need in the material realm.

Rejoice in Me, trust in Me, share all of your life with Me, see Me in everything, take delight in Me. Share everything with Me just as a child shares her pains and cuts and sorrows and newfound treasures and joys and small accomplishments with her mother.

And give Me the joy of sharing everything with you.

MAY 5
LET ME CHOOSE

My loved ones. Yes, people should think of Me with their hearts, not only their heads, and then worship would naturally follow.

Breathe in My very Spirit in pure air and heart-felt desire.

Always keep the eye of your spirit gazing upon Me, the window of your soul always open to Me. You must be constantly aware that all things are yours — that I delight to give you what is lovely.

Rid your mind of any thought that limits. You can have whatever is beautiful. Leave the choice to Me more and more. You will have no regrets.

MAY 6
MAGNIFICENT BOLDNESS

The journey is long and weary. It is a weary world. So many today are exhausted. "Come to me, all you who are weary and burdened, and I will give you rest" (Matthew 11:28 NIV 1984).

My children who gather and live up under My flag, you must see these words are inscribed upon it: "the Son of Man."

Whatever the world is feeling, I must feel, I — the Son of Man. You are My followers. Therefore, the weariness felt by people today must also be shared by you. Those who are weary and carry heavy burdens must come to *you* and find the same rest that you found in Me.

My children, My followers should not focus on sitting at a seat of honor to My right or to My left, but to be prepared to drink from the bitter cup from which I drink (Mark 10:35–40).

Poor world — teach it that there is only one cure for every suffering — unity with Me. Dare to suffer. Dare to conquer. Be filled with My magnificent boldness. Remember that. Declare that even what seems beyond your grasp is yours.

The very thing that the world would think impossible can always be yours. Remember, My children, magnificent boldness.

MAY 7
AGAINST THE TIDE

A man rowing a boat, trusting in Me, does not lean on his oars and drift with the tide, trusting the current to take him to his destination.

No, more often — once I have shown the way — you must direct all your efforts against the tide. And even when difficulties arise, it is by your effort that they will be overcome. But while doing so, you can always have strength and joy through Me.

My fishermen-disciples did not find the fish already in their nets on the shore (Luke 5:1–11)! I take man's effort and bless that. I require man's effort and he needs My blessing. It is this partnership that means success.

MAY 8
THE REST OF GOD

I lead you. The way is clear. Go forward unafraid. I am beside you. Listen, listen, listen to My voice. My hand is controlling everything.

Remember that I can work through you better when you are at rest. Go very slowly, very quietly, from one task to the next — taking time to rest and pray in between.

Do not be too busy. Do things in the order I tell you. The rest of God is in a realm beyond all man's activities. Go there often, and you will indeed find peace and joy.

All work that results from resting with God is miracle-work. Claim the power to work miracles, both of you.

Know that you can do all things through Christ who gives you strength (Philippians 4:13). No! Even more than that, know that you can do all things through Christ who gives you rest.

MAY 9
HARMONY WITHIN

Follow My guidance. Be afraid to head out alone, just like a child is afraid to leave her mother's side. Doubting your own wisdom and relying on Mine will teach you humility.

Humility is not being critical of your "self." It is forgetting the self. No, more than that, it is forgetting the self because you are remembering Me.

You must not expect to live in a world where everything is in perfect harmony. You must not expect to live where others always agree with you. Your job is to keep peace in your heart during difficult circumstances. Harmony is always yours when you strain your ear to catch heaven's music.

Always doubt your power or wisdom to make things right. Ask Me to fix everything. Leave it to Me, and go on your way loving and laughing. I am wisdom. Only My wisdom can correctly decide anything, settle any problem. So, rely on Me. All is well.

MAY 10
CALM — NOT SPEED

"... in quietness and trust is your strength."
(ISAIAH 30:15 NIV 1984)

All agitation is destructive of good, while all calm is constructive of good, and at the same time, destructive of evil.

When man wants evil destroyed, so often he rushes into action. That is wrong. First, "be still and know that I am God" (Psalm 46:10a NIV 1984). Then act only as I tell you. With God, there is always calmness. Calmness is trust in action. Simply trust; perfect trust can keep you calm.

Never be afraid of any circumstances or difficulties which help you to develop this calm. Just as the world has to learn speed in order to achieve, you have to learn calm. All great work for Me is done first in the soul of the individual worker.

MAY 11
THE DIVINE THIRD

When I have led you through these storms, there will be other words for you, other messages — other guidance.

Your friendship is so deep, and your desire to love Me, follow Me, and serve Me is so great that soon, when this time of difficulty is over, to be alone together will always mean to be hidden away with Me.

There are few friendships in the world like that in spite of the fact that while I was on earth, I taught My disciples, just as I am teaching you, the power of *two together* (Mark 6:7).

And now tonight, I have more to say to you. I say that the time is coming, is here even now, when those who visit you two together will know that I am the Divine Third in your friendship.

MAY 12
THRILL OF PROTECTION

Rid yourself of all thoughts of doubt or trouble. Never tolerate them for a single second. Bar the windows and doors of your souls against them as you would bar your home against a thief who would break in to steal your treasures.

What greater treasures can you have than peace and rest and joy? And these are all stolen from you by doubt and fear and despair.

Face each day with love and laughter. Face the storm.

Joy. Peace. Love. These are My great gifts. Follow Me to find all three. I want you to feel the thrill of protection and safety now. Anyone can feel this while in a harbor, but real joy and victory come only to those who sense these while riding out a storm.

Say, "All is well." But don't say it as if you were repeating empty words. Use it as you would use a healing ointment for a cut or a wound until the poison has been drawn out; *then*, use it until the sore is healed; *then*, until the thrill of fresh life floods your being.

All is well.

MAY 13
NEVER JUDGE

What joy follows self-conquest! You cannot conquer and control others, either of you, until you have completely conquered yourselves.

Can you picture yourselves being absolutely immovable? Think about when I was before the mocking soldiers, being beaten, spit upon, and yet never saying a word — *never a word* (Matthew 27:27–31). Try to understand that as divine power. Remember, only by the power of perfect silence, perfect self-control, can you prove your right to be in charge.

Never judge (Matthew 7:1). The heart of man is so delicate, so complex, only its Maker can know it. Each heart is so different, driven by different motives, controlled by different circumstances, influenced by different hardships and hurts.

How can one person judge another? Leave to Me the unraveling of the puzzles of life. Leave to Me the teaching of understanding. Bring each heart to Me, its Maker, and leave it with Me secure in the certainty that everything which is wrong, I can set right.

MAY 14
LOVE'S PURSUIT

Remember that this loving Master delights in the intimacy of demands made upon Him, as much as He desires His followers and friends to delight in the tender intimacy of *His* demands upon them.

The wonder of family life is expressed in the freedom with which a child makes demands and claims upon his parents. Such wonder is just as beautifully expressed in the freedom of his parents to make loving demands to share in the love and joy of their children.

Intimacy comes only as the result of frequent conversations with Me, many prayers to Me, and listening to and obeying My instructions. It is that intimacy which makes My followers bold enough to approach Me as one friend to another.

In all things, submit to My tender urging, but remember, I also submit to yours. Do not ask only for the big things I have said can be yours, but also ask for the little tender signs of love. Remember that I came as the world's great love. Never think of My love as only tender compassion and forgiveness. It is that, but it is also the love of a suitor who shows His love by countless words and actions and by tender thoughts.

Remember, there is God in each of you, too, through the indwelling of the Holy Spirit (Acts 4:31). So as a person grows to be more and more like My Father in heaven, I bring to our friendship a reverent, tender love. I see, as no man can see, the indwelling Spirit in you.

A man so often will see in his fellow man those desires and qualities he possesses himself. So only I, being the one true God, can recognize the God in man. Also remember this in your dealings with others.

Your motives and goals can only be understood by those who have achieved the same spiritual maturity as you have. So do not uselessly, foolishly, expect understanding from others. Do not unfairly criticize them for their lack of understanding, for it is like you are speaking a foreign language to them.

MAY 15
FIRST THE SPIRITUAL

What can I say to you? Your heart is broken. Then remember, "He heals the brokenhearted" (Psalm 147:3a NIV 1984). Just feel the tenderness of My hands as I bind up your wounds (Psalm 147:3).

You are very privileged, both of you. I share My plans and secrets with you, and make My purposes known to you, while so many others have to feel their way in the dark.

Try to depend on these words: "Seek first the kingdom of God and His righteousness, and all these things shall be added to you" (Matthew 6:33 NKJV). Therefore, do not strive for material things, but strive tirelessly for the things of My kingdom.

This is so strange to you human beings. You believe that the material things should come first, and only after you obtain those would you grow in the knowledge of spiritual things. That is not so in My kingdom. Spiritual things must come before the material. In order to obtain your material needs, redouble your efforts to acquire the spiritual.

MAY 16
PRAY AND PRAISE

You may come to Me often with all of your pleas because I know that only in your heartfelt prayers, and in the calm trust that follows, do you learn strength and gain peace. Therefore, I have made it an obligation of My disciples to engage in continuous, persistent petition.

Never get tired of praying. One day, when man sees how marvelously his prayers have been answered, then he will deeply, so deeply, regret that he prayed so little.

Prayer changes everything. Prayer re-creates. Prayer is irresistible. Pray, literally without ceasing (1 Thessalonians 5:17).

Pray until trust is such a firm foundation in your life that it seems almost unnecessary to pray, and then pray on because it has become so much of a habit that you cannot resist it.

And always pray until prayer merges into praise. That is the only note on which true prayer should end. The love and laughter of your attitude toward people is reflected in the prayer and praise of your attitude toward God.

MAY 17
SORROW TO JOY

Weeping may last through the night, but joy comes with the morning" (Psalm 30:5 NLT).

My bravest children are those who can anticipate the morning, enduring the night of sorrow while feeling the underlying joy that gives proof of their confident expectations of the morning.

MAY 18
NEW AND VITAL POWER

Let all the world look to me for salvation!" (Isaiah 45:22a NLT). Salvation is not a matter of merit, of earning it. The promise was for everyone who looked.

Everyone has the power to look. One look is enough. Salvation follows (Numbers 21:9).

Look, and you are saved from despair. Look, and you are saved from trouble. Look, and you are saved from worry. Look, and into you there flows a peace beyond all understanding (Philippians 4:7), a new and vital power, a joy which is wonderful indeed.

Look and keep looking. Doubt flees, joy reigns, and hope conquers.

Life, eternal life, is yours — revitalizing, renewing.

MAY 19
RESCUED AND GUIDED

Rest knowing everything is so safe in My hands. Rest is trust. Constant activity is distrust. Because you do not know that I am working for you, you do not rest. Inactivity when you lack that knowledge is the result of despair, not trust.

"[My] arm is not too weak to save you ..." (Isaiah 59:1a NLT). Know that. Repeat it. Rely on it.

Welcome that knowledge. Delight in it. This truth is like hope thrown out to a drowning man. Each time you repeat it, it is like pulling him one step closer to the shore and safety.

Let that illustration teach you a great truth. Lay hold of the truth, pray it, affirm it, hold onto the rope. Your attempts to save yourself are so foolish, with one hand on the rope and the other making efforts to swim ashore! You may let go of the rope and make it more difficult for the rescuer — who then has to act even more cautiously so that he doesn't lose you.

Life does not consist only of storms and chaos. The Psalmist who said "all your waves and breakers have swept over me" (Psalm 42:7 NIV 1984), also wrote, "He lifted me out of the pit of despair, out of the mud and the mire. He set my feet on solid ground and steadied me as I walked along" (Psalm 40:2 NLT).

Think about that wonderful truth, the three steps of safety, security, and guidance.

1. "He lifted me out of the pit of despair" — *Safety*.

2. "He set my feet on solid ground" — *Security*.

3. "He steadied me as I walked along" — *Guidance*. Guidance is the final stage when the saved soul trusts Me so completely that it no longer seeks its own way but leaves all future plans to Me, its rescuer.

MAY 20
WIN ME — WIN ALL

You will conquer. The conquering spirit is never crushed. Keep a brave and trusting heart. Face all of your difficulties in the spirit of conquest.

Rise to greater heights than you have ever known before. Remember where I am, there is victory. Forces of evil, inside of you and outside of you, flee at My presence.

Win *Me* and all is won. *All.*

MAY 21
LEAVE IT AT MY FEET

To see Me, you must bring Me your troubles and show Me your heart of trust. Then, as you leave your cares with Me, you become aware of My presence.

Being persistently aware of My presence brings its reward of Me. No man may see My face through a cloud of worry. Only when the burden is left at My feet do you pass on to awareness and spiritual sight.

Remember: obedience, obedience, obedience — the narrow and difficult way into the kingdom (Matthew 7:14).

Never let it be said of you, even in lovingly tender correction, "Why do you call Me 'Lord, Lord,' and not do the things which I say?" (Luke 6:46 NKJV).

Character is chiseled into beauty by daily discipline, and daily duties done. For, in many ways, My disciples must work out their own salvation, though this is not possible without My strength and help, and without talking it over with Me.

Even for the spiritual life, the training is different for different spirits. The man who would gladly live a life of prayer and meditation is forced into the busyness of life, and the busy man is asked to rest and wait patiently for Me. Oh, joy. Oh, rest. And in the busyness of life, always be at peace.

MAY 22
COMMAND YOUR LORD

Lord, I claim Your help.

Yes! Claim, be constantly claiming. There is a trust that waits a long time, and a trust that will not tolerate any delay. Once it is convinced it is on the right course, once it is sure of God's guidance, this impatient trust says, with all the persistence of a child, *"Now!"* "Do not delay, O my God" (Psalm 40:17 NKJV).

You are no longer servants, but friends (John 15:15). As a friend, you can command your friend — can know that all your friend, the true friend, has is yours by right. That does not mean taking advantage of that friend, but claiming that friend's resources — the authority of his name, time, and all that he has — when your supply is exhausted.

Friendship — true friendship — implies the right to claim. There is perfect freedom in God's service. You are heirs of God — you are joint heirs with Me in the inheritance (Romans 8:17). We share the Father's property. You have the same right to use it and claim it as I have. Use your right. A beggar begs. Sons and daughters claim.

No wonder when I see My children sitting outside of My house waiting and begging, I leave them there until they realize how foolish they are being, when all they have to do is to walk into their home and help themselves to whatever is there.

Not everyone can have this outlook. There must first be the definite realization that you are sons and daughters of God.

MAY 23
LITTLE WORRIES

Your lack of control is not due to the *big* burdens, but to your permitting the *little* worries and troubles and burdens to add up.

If anything bothers you, deal with that and make that right with Me before you allow yourself to speak to or meet with anyone, or to undertake any new responsibility.

More and more, think of yourself as performing My errands and then coming back quickly to Me to tell Me the message has been delivered, the task is done.

Then, with no feeling of responsibility as to the result (your only responsibility was to get the job done), go out again rejoicing that there is still more you can do for My sake.

MAY 24
ABUNDANCE

The world goes on around you, not seeing you. Not knowing about your heartaches and troubles, your battles won, your victories, your difficulties.

But be thankful, both of you, that there is One who knows, One who takes note of every crisis, every effort, every heartache.

For you both, who are not merely listeners to the Word (James 1:22), you must know that every troubled soul I tell you about is someone for you to help. You must help everyone you can. You do not help enough. As you help others, help will flow back to you, and your circle of helpfulness will widen more and more, ever more and more.

Think of yourselves as two of My disciples who are present at the feeding of the five thousand (Matthew 14:13–21). Imagine that I hand the food to you, and you pass it on, and ever more and more. With so few loaves and only two fish, you can always say, "We only have enough for our own needs." It was not only My blessing, but the passing-on by the disciples that worked the miracle.

Get a feeling of generous giving into yourselves. They were all filled (Luke 9:17). There was an oversupply.

I give with a large hand and heart. Remember the miraculous catch of fish (Luke 5:1–11). The nets broke; the boats began to sink with the lavishness of My gift. Forget all limitations.

Abundance is God's supply. Reject all limited thoughts. Receive showers of blessings and, in turn, shower blessings on others.

MAY 25
ACCOMPLISH ANYTHING

There will be no limit to what you can accomplish. Realize that. Never give up on any task or abandon the thought of any task because it seems beyond your power, unless you see the task is not My will for you. This I command you.

Think of a tiny flower shoot in the hard, winter ground. There is no certainty that even when it has forced its weary way up, sunlight and warmth will greet it.

This must seem to be a task beyond its power. But with the inner urge of life within the seed compelling it, it carries out that task. The kingdom of heaven is like this.

CLAIM MORE

You are doing your claiming as I have instructed you, and soon you will see the result. You cannot do this for long without it being seen in the material. It is an undying law.

Right now, you are like children practicing a new skill. Practice — practice — soon you will be able to do it so easily.

You see results in other people's lives being manifested so easily, see them demonstrating My power so effortlessly. But you have not seen the discipline they have gone through. Discipline that is absolutely necessary before this power is given to My disciples. It is another initiation.

You are feeling that you have learned so much that your life cannot be a failure. That is correct, but others have to wait to see the outward manifestation in your lives before they realize this spiritual truth.

MAY 27
ROOTS AND FRUITS

Remember another lesson to be learned from a seed. It sends a shoot down so that it may be rooted and grounded, while at the same time it sends a shoot up to be the plant and flower that will bring joy to the world.

Growing both ways is necessary. Without the strong root, the plant would soon wither. Similarly, many efforts fail to yield results due to a lack of growth in Me. The higher the growth, the deeper the roots must be.

Many people forget this. Therefore, their work does not have any permanent results for Me. Beware of the leaves and flowers without the strong root.

MAY 28
TEST YOUR LOVE

A great love knows that in every difficulty, every trial, every failure, the presence of a loved one is enough. Test your love for Me by this.

Just to be with Me, just to know that I am beside you — does that bring you joy and peace? If not, then the smallness of your love for Me, and your failure to realize My love for you, are to blame.

Then, if that is so, pray for more love.

MAY 29
FORGET

Regret nothing. Not even your sins and failures. When a man stands on top of a mountain and views the magnificent creation below, he does not spend his energy dwelling on each time he failed or fainted, or on the stones and stumbles that marked his upward climb.

This must be true of you. Breathe in the rich blessings of each new day — forget everything that is behind you.

Man is made so that he can carry the weight of twenty-four hours, no more. Carrying the burden of past years weighs a man down, and if you add the burden of the days to come, his back will break. I have promised to help you with the burden of today only. I have taken the past from you. If you, foolish hearts, choose to pick up that burden and carry it, then you insult Me indeed if you expect Me to share it.

Each day ends for better or worse. What you must face when you wake up is what must be lived: the coming twenty-four hours.

A soldier on a march carries only what he needs. Would you feel sorry for him if you saw him also bearing the overwhelming weight of the worn-out shoes and uniforms of past marches and years? And yet, in the mental and spiritual life, people do these things. It is little wonder that My poor world is heartsick and weary.

You must not do this.

MAY 30
THE DEVIL'S DEATH KNELL

Our Lord, we praise You.

Praise is the devil's death knell, the sure sign of his destruction. Resignation, acceptance of My will, obedience to it — none of these have the power to defeat evil the way that praise has.

The joyful heart is My best weapon against all evil. Oh, pray and praise!

You are learning your lesson. You are being led into a large place. Go with songs of rejoicing. Rejoice more and more. You will be happy indeed if each day has its thrill of joy.

Talk to Me more during the day. Look up into My face — a look of love, a feeling of security, a thrill of joy at sensing the closeness of My presence — these are your best prayers.

Allow these to let the day's work go more smoothly; then fear will vanish. And it is fear that is the grim figure which prevents success.

MAY 31
PRAYER WITHOUT WORDS

Lord, hear us, we pray.

I hear and I answer. Spend a lot of time in prayer. There are many kinds of prayer, but whatever kind, prayer is the joining of your soul and mind and heart to God.

Even if it is only a glance toward heaven in faith, a look or word of love, or confidence, even without a prayer being spoken, it still follows that your supply and all that is necessary are secured.

This is true because the soul being joined to God and united with Him receives all things in and through Him. And the soul, while still in human form, also needs the things belonging to its earthly dwelling.

JUNE 1
COMPANIONSHIP

The way that a soul is transformed is by walking with Me.

It is not so much asking Me to make you "this" or "that," but the living with Me, thinking of Me, talking to Me — that is how you grow to be like Me.

Love Me. Rest in Me.

Rejoice in Me.

JUNE 2
MY IMAGE

Our Lord and our God, we praise
You, we bless You, we worship You.
Make us to be like You.

You are willing to drink from "the bitter cup of suffering" (Matthew 20:22 NLT) from which I drink — the wine of sorrow and disappointment.

You are Mine, and both of you will grow to be more and more like Me, your Master.

It is as true today as it was in the days of Moses that no man can see My face and live (Exodus 33:20).

The self, who you were before you knew Jesus, shrivels up and dies, and My image is stamped on your soul.

JUNE 3
EJECT SIN WITH LOVE

*Our Lord, we love You and
praise You. You are our joy and
our exceedingly great reward.*

Remember that love is the power that transforms the world. Not only love for Me, not only love for the few dear to you, but love for everyone — tax collectors, sinners, prostitutes — *love.*

It is the only weapon with which sin can be driven out. Drive out sin with love.

Drive out fear, depression, despair, and a sense of failure with praise.

Praise is acknowledging what I sent you. Few people would send another gift before they had received acknowledgement of the first one. Therefore, praise (acknowledging My gift and blessing) opens the way for Me to shower more blessings on the thankful heart.

Learn to do this just as a child learns to say "Thank you" as a courtesy with perhaps no real sense of gratitude at all. Do this until, at last, a thrill of joy, of thankful awe, accompanies the spoken word.

Do not expect to feel the same way you know others feel or have felt. Continue on the arid way of obedience, and your persistence will be rewarded when you come to the spring, the glad spring of water (John 4:14).

Oh, rejoice in Me and, as much as you are able, spread joy to everyone around you.

JUNE 4
DIVINE PATIENCE

Lord, make us like You. Mold us into Your image.

Molding, My children, means cutting and chiseling. It means sacrificing the personal to conform to the ideal. It is not only My work but yours as well.

Your task is to quickly recognize the selfishness in your desires and motives, actions, words, and thoughts, and then to immediately appeal to Me for help to eliminate that selfishness.

It is a work that requires cooperation — Mine and yours. It is a work that also brings a great sense of failure and discouragement at times, because as the work proceeds, you see more and more clearly all that remains yet to be done.

Shortcomings of which you had barely been aware or for which you were not the least bit sorry, now make you troubled and heartsick.

Courage. That in itself is a sign of progress.

Have patience, not only with others, but each of you with yourself.

As you see the slowness of the upward progress you are making, in spite of your best efforts and your struggles, you will gain a divine patience with others whose imperfections bother you.

So you must go onward and upward. Forward. Patience — Perseverance — Struggle. Remember that I am beside you, your Captain and your Helper. I am so tender, so patient, so strong.

Yes, we cooperate, and as I share your troubles, failures, difficulties, and heartaches, so likewise, you, being My friends, share My patience and My strength. You are My beloved.

THAT TENDER VOICE

I speak very quietly. Listen to My voice. Pay no attention to the voices of the world—only the tender divine voice.

Listen and you will never be disappointed. Listen, and your anxious thoughts and tired nerves will be calmed. The voice divine—not so much in strength as in tenderness. Not so much in power as in restfulness.

But the tenderness and the restfulness will heal your scars and make you strong. Then it is your responsibility to let all your power be My power at work in and through you. Man's little power is like clay compared to the granite rock of My power.

I care about you so much. Never feel like you are at the world's mercy. Angels guard you day and night, and nothing can harm you. You would certainly thank Me if only you knew about the darts of worry and evildoing My angels prevent from reaching you.

Thank Me indeed for dangers which are unknown—unseen—but avoided because they have been turned away.

HOW PEOPLE SEE ME

I came to help a world. Each person has different needs. Accordingly, each person sees Me differently.

It is not necessary that you see Me as others see Me — not the world, nor even the church, My disciples or My followers. But, it is necessary that *you* see Me, each of you, as supplying all that *you* personally need.

The weak need My strength. The strong need My tenderness. The tempted and the fallen need My salvation. The righteous need My pity for sinners. The lonely need a friend. The fighters need a leader.

No man could be all of these things to men — only God could be. In every one of My relationships to man, you must see God: the God-Friend, the God-Leader, the God-Savior.

JUNE 7
TRUE BEAUTY

"Incline your ear, and come to Me.
Hear, and your soul shall live."
(ISAIAH 55:3 NKJV)

Do not merely live in grace and power and beauty. Grow in grace and power and beauty — the true beauty, the beauty of holiness.

Always strive for the things of My kingdom.

In the animal kingdom, an animal can alter its very form to allow it to reach that which it delights to eat. In the same way, reaching for the treasures of My kingdom, your whole nature changes so that you can best enjoy and receive the wonders of that kingdom.

Dwell on these truths.

JUNE 8
THE ONLY WAY

Down through the ages, it is My power alone which has kept millions of souls brave and true and strong who would otherwise have fallen by the wayside.

The faith has been kept alive and handed down, not by those who lived an easy life, but by those who struggled and suffered and died for Me.

This life is not for the body, it is for the soul. Too often, people choose the way of life that best suits the body, not the way that best suits the soul. And I permit only what best suits the soul.

If you accept this, a wonderful transformation results. If you reject it, My purpose is frustrated, your best prayer is unanswered, progress — spiritual progress — is delayed, and trouble and grief are stored up.

Each of you must try to picture your soul as a separate being to be trained by us — by you and Me. Then you will share, gladly share, in the discipline and training.

Stand apart from your soul with Me and welcome training — rejoice at progress.

JUNE 9
AN OBSTACLE RACE

Rise above your fears and desires into My joy. It is enough to heal all your hurts and wounds. Forget all sense of failure and all of your shortcomings, and all the painful jolts and jars of life. And trust Me, love Me, call upon Me.

Your discipleship is an obstacle race. "So run to win!" (1 Corinthians 9:24b NLT). Win not only your hearts' desires, but win Me—your souls' joy and haven.

What would you think of a runner who threw himself on the ground in despair at the first hurdle he faced?

So, over, and on, and up! I am your leader and your goal.

JUNE 10
THE DAY OF TROUBLE

"Make thankfulness your sacrifice to
God, and keep the vows you made to
the Most High. Then call on me when
you are in trouble, and I will rescue
you, and you will give me glory."
(PSALM 50:14–15 NLT)

To praise and thank and steadily keep your vows to Me is like placing coins in My bank from which, with confidence and certainty, you can make withdrawals in your time of need. Remember that.

The world wonders when it sees a man unexpectedly withdraw large and surprising amounts from his bank for his own needs, the needs of a friend, or for some charity.

But what the world has not seen are the countless small deposits into that bank, earned by faithful work in many ways.

And so it is in My kingdom. The world sees a man of faith make a sudden demand upon Me, upon My resources, and that demand is met!

The world thinks that the man has magical powers. No! What the world did not see was that the man had been paying in faithfully and steadily — in thanks and praise, and by promises fulfilled.

It is the same way with you, My children. "Make thankfulness your sacrifice to God, and keep the vows you made to the Most High. Then call on me when you are in trouble, and I will rescue you, and you will give me glory."

This is a promise for the boring days when it seems like very little is happening, and to cheer you up, My children. When you do not seem to be able to do big things, you can be storing your little acts and words of faithfulness in My great storehouse, so that they are ready to be withdrawn on the day you make your big demand.

JUNE 11
MY MARK!

O Lord, we thank You for
Your great gift of peace.

My gift is the peace which only I can give in the midst of a restless world surrounded by trouble and difficulty. To know that peace is to be imprinted with the stamp of the kingdom — the mark of the Lord Jesus Christ. My mark.

When you have learned that peace, you are able to evaluate real values, the values of the kingdom and the values of all the world has to offer.

That peace is loving faith at rest.

JUNE 12
HOUSE ON A ROCK

Listen carefully for My voice and obey Me instantly. Obedience is your great sign of faith. "Why are you so polite with me, always saying, 'Yes, sir,' and 'That's right, sir,' but never doing the thing I tell you?" (Luke 6:46 MSG). That's what I said when

I was on earth to the many people who followed Me and heard Me, but did not do what I said.

I compared the man who heard and did not do to the man who built his house on the sand. During storms and times of trouble, he is destroyed; his house falls. (Luke 6:49).

I compared the man who unfailingly obeyed Me to the man who built his house upon a rock. During the storms, he is steady, immovable (Luke 6:47–48).

By this, I do not mean that you must only keep My commandments or even live by the teachings of My Sermon on the Mount. I mean more than that to those who know Me intimately. I mean that in all things, you must follow the inner guiding that I give, the little instructions I speak to each individual soul, the wishes I make known to you — and desire to have carried out.

The secure, steadfast, immovable life of My disciples, the rock home, is not built by wishing or in a moment, but is laid, stone by stone, foundations, walls, and roof, by the acts of obedience, carrying out My wishes day by day, the loving doing of My will.

"Therefore everyone who hears these words of mine and puts them into practice is like a wise man who built his house on the rock. The rain came down, the streams rose, and the winds blew and beat against that house; yet it did not fall, because it had its foundation on the rock" (Matthew 7:24–25 NIV 1984).

That rock home, man-made but divinely inspired — the house of obedience — is the truest expression of a disciple's adoration and worship — it is *there* I come to dwell with My loved one.

Am I not giving you both work and hope? Work for the gray days? Just little plain bricks of duties done, and of My wishes carried out. All of them strengthen you and make your character into that steadfast, immovable Christian character of which My servant Paul spoke and which he urged his followers to have (1 Corinthians 15:58).

JUNE 13
GOD-INSPIRED

You have now started climbing a mountain. The steps going up are steep, but your power to help others will be truly marvelous.

You will not go up alone. Everyone to whom you send out loving, sympathetic thoughts will be helped upward by you.

When you look to Me, all your thoughts are God-inspired. Act on those thoughts, and you will be led forward. They are not your own impulses but the prompting of My Spirit. When you obey them, they will bring the answers to your prayers.

Love and trust. Do not let any unkind thoughts about anyone dwell in your hearts. Then I can act with all of the power of My Spirit without interference.

JUNE 14
FACE TODAY WITH ME

*Our Lord and our God. Make us
all you would have us to be.*

It is not circumstances that need to change first, but yourselves, and then the conditions will naturally change. Make every effort to become all that I would have you to be. Follow My every leading. I am your only guide.

Try to put every troubling thought out of your mind. Take each day and, without looking backward, face the day's problems with Me — seek My help and guidance about what you can do.

Never look back and never leave until tomorrow that for which you can get My guidance today.

GLORY, GLORY DAWNS

I am planning for you. My ways are wonderful beyond your knowing.

Oh! Realize My generosity and My goodness more and more. The wonder of being led by Me! The beauty of a guided life!

These will enter your consciousness more and more, and bring you joy ever more and more.

You are nearly at the point when you will ask in My name for whatever you want, and it will be given to you (John 16:23b).

You have entered a wonderful era — your lives are planned and blessed by Me as never before.

You are overcoming all adversity. You are counting all things as worthless if you can win Me (Philippians 3:8). And the promises to him who overcomes are truly wonderful,* and will always be fulfilled.

*See Revelation 2:7, 11, 17, 26–28; 3:5, 12; and 21:7.

SEEK ME EARLY

Walk in My way and trust Me. No evil can touch you. I am yours just as certainly as you are Mine. Rest in that truth.

Rest, which means to cease all struggle. Gain a calm, strong confidence in that certainty. Do not rest in Me only when the world's struggles prove to be too much to handle and too many for you to bear or face alone. Rest in Me when you need perfect understanding, when you need the awareness of tender, loving friendship and communication.

The world, My poor world, runs to Me when its difficulties are too great to be overcome in any other way. The world forgets, or never realizes, that if, with the same eagerness, those hearts sought Me merely for companionship and loving interaction, many of the difficulties would not arise.

The circumstances, the life, the character would be so altered — so purified — that those same difficulties would not exist.

Seek Me *early*; that is the way to find Me. *Early*, before I get crowded out by life's troubles and difficulties and pleasures.

JUNE 17
DEAR NAME

Jesus. Say My name often. It was in My name Peter commanded the lame man to walk. "In the name of Jesus Christ of Nazareth, get up and walk" (Acts 3:6b NLT).

"Jesus." Merely saying My name in love and tenderness drives away all evil. It is the word before which all the evil hosts flee (Acts 16:16–18).

"Jesus." My name is the call for a lifeline to rescue you from temptation.

"Jesus." The name banishes loneliness and dispels gloom.

"Jesus." It calls for help to overcome your faults.

"I will protect those who trust in my name" (Psalm 91:14 NLT).

Yes! My name — "Jesus." Use it more. Use it tenderly. Use it prayerfully. Use it powerfully.

The world always seems to think that serving Me means that you have to be doing something. Only those who are close to Me have seen that living a life apart, a life of prayer, may and so often does accomplish more than all the service man can offer Me.

If man lived apart with Me and only went out to serve at My direct command, My Spirit could perform more and accomplish truly mighty things.

Follow the path of obedience. It leads to the throne of God. Your treasure might be material success which is necessary to further the work of My kingdom. Or it might be the hidden spiritual wonders revealed by Me only to those who diligently seek Me. Whatever it is, your treasure lies at the end of that path.

From one point (a promise of Mine or a command) to the next, you have to follow the path of obedience until you finally reach the success you crave.

For now, all *your* work is in the material world, and the spiritual is only to help the material. When your material goal is reached, then the material will only serve to obtain the spiritual.

JUNE 20
MIRACLES AGAIN

Wait to hear My will and then obey. At all costs, obey.

Do not fear. I am a wall of protection around you. See this. To see this with the eyes of faith is to cause it to become real in the material.

Remember, I yearn to work miracles just as I did when I performed them during My time on earth. But the same condition holds true today: there are many mighty works that I cannot do because of unbelief (Mark 6:5).

So it is only in response to your belief that I can work miracles now.

JUNE 21
SEE AS I SEE

O Lord, we praise You.
Bless us, we beg You.

I bless you. I promise you freedom. Rejoice in Me. You shall be shielded from the storm.

Wonders have unfolded. Just to come before Me and stay for a while in My presence — this must strengthen you and help you.

Let Me teach you (Matthew 11:29). The only way for so many in My poor world to keep calm, to stay sane, is to "have the same mindset as Christ Jesus" (Philippians 2:5 NIV 2011). My mindset.

That mindset is one you can never obtain by reasoning or by reading, but only by living with Me and sharing My life.

Think about Me often. Talk about Me often. See others as I see them. Let nothing less satisfy you.

JUNE 22
YOUR RED SEA

Go forward fearlessly.

Do not think about the Red Sea (Exodus 13:17—14:31) that lies ahead.

Rest assured that when you come to it, the waters will part and you will cross over to your promised land of freedom.

JUNE 23
CLING TO ME

Cling to Me until the life from Me (the divine life) flows into your being through that very contact and revives your fainting spirit.

Become recharged. When you are tired, do what I did on earth: *Sit by the well* (John 4:6). *Rest.*

Rest and gain power and strength, and the work, also, will come to you just as it came to Me (John 4:7–42).

Rest until every worry has gone, and then let the tide of love and joy flow in.

JUNE 24
WHEN GUIDANCE TAKES ITS TIME

As I prompt you — act. When you have no clear guidance, then go forward quietly along the path of duty I have laid before you.

No fear, no panic, just quietly doing your daily duty.

This attitude of faith will receive its reward, in the same way as acting upon My direct guidance is rewarded.

Rejoice in the sense of security that is yours.

JUNE 25
GOD'S FRIENDSHIP

I am your friend. Your companion on the dreary ways of life.

I take away the grayness and horror from those ways. I transform them. Even in human friendships, the routine way, the weary way, the steep way may all seem like heavenly roads if the presence of a beloved friend transforms them.

Let your hearts and minds be wrapped in the Sabbath calm. Let it be a rest from the worries and concerns of life, a stop along the busy highway when you seek some rest and shade.

Have you ever realized the wonder of the friendship you can have with Me? Have you ever considered what it means to be able to summon, at will, the God of the world?

Even when a privileged visitor goes to see an earthly king, he must first wait in the palace anteroom, and may only enter when it pleases the king.

But I have given My subjects the right to enter My presence whenever they desire. More than that, they can summon Me to a bedside or a workshop, and I am there.

Is there anything more divine love could do? Your closest friend on earth cannot be with you instantly. But I, your Lord, your Master, your Friend — I can!

When men seek to worship Me, they think of the worlds I rule over, of creation, of mighty law and order — and then they feel the awe that precedes worship.

To you I say feel awe, feel the desire to worship Me in wondering amazement. But also consider the mighty, tender, humble way I come down to you to be your Friend. Think of Me in the little everyday things of life.

JUNE 26
DO NOT RUSH

In the little daily things of life, learn to delay doing anything until you have received My guidance.

So many people's lives lack balance. That is because they ask for My help for momentous decisions and the big things in life, but rush alone into the small things.

Remember that the people around you are most often annoyed or attracted by what you do in the small things.

JUNE 27
NO SELF-CONDEMNATION

The eternal arms shelter you. "Underneath are the everlasting arms" (Deuteronomy 33:27 NIV 1984). This is a promise to those who rise above earthly concerns and seek to soar higher to the kingdom of heaven.

You must not carry the burden of your failure. Go on in faith. The clouds will clear, and the way will lighten—the path becomes less stony with every step you take. "So run to win!" (1 Corinthians

9:24b NLT). If you strictly perform the simple duties, success will crown your efforts.

I had no words of condemnation for anyone I healed. The paraplegic I healed was made whole and free, even though he had wrecked his body by sin (Mark 2:1–5).

The woman at the well was not overwhelmed by My saying, "You've had five husbands, and the man you are living with now isn't even your husband" (John 4:18 MSG).

The woman caught committing adultery was told, "Neither do I condemn you; go and sin no more" (John 8:11 NKJV). She was not told to bear the burden of the knowledge of her sin …

Remember, three things will last forever — faith, hope, and love (1 Corinthians 13:13a). Faith is your attitude towards Me. Love is your attitude toward your fellow man, but equally necessary is hope, which is confidence in yourself to succeed.

JUNE 28
TABLE OF DELIGHTS

This time of training and teaching has not been useless. The time of suppression, repression, and depression is now changed into a time of glorious expression!

Life is flooded through and through with joy and gladness. Indeed, I have prepared a table of delights, a feast of all good things for you (Psalm 23:5).

Indeed, your cup runs over and now you can truly feel from the bottom of your heart, "Surely goodness and mercy shall follow me all the days of my life; and I will dwell in the house of the Lord forever" (Psalm 23:6 NKJV).

JUNE 29
MY WILL — YOUR JOY

Our Lord and our God, lead us, we beg You.
Lead us and keep us.

You can never go where My love and care cannot reach you. Remember that. "Evil can't get close to you" (Psalm 91:10a MSG). I only allow and use the circumstances which are right for you.

But I know that the first step is always to lay your will down before Me as an offering, happily knowing that I shall do what is best for you. Rest assured that if you trust Me, whatever I do for you will be the best.

Your second step is to be sure, and tell Me so, that: first, I am powerful enough to do everything ("The king's heart is like a stream of water directed by the Lord; he guides it wherever he pleases," Proverbs 21:1 NLT); and second, that no miracle is impossible with Me. With God all things are possible—and I and My Father are one (Matthew 19:26; John 10:30)!

Then leave everything to Me. Be happy that you can leave all of your responsibilities in the Master's hand. Be assured of safety and protection. Remember, you cannot see the future. I can.

You could not stand it. So I can only reveal it to you little by little. Accept My will, and it will bring you joy.

JUNE 30
UNDERSTAND THEM

Take joy wherever you go. You have been very blessed. You are being very blessed.

There are so many blessings that are awaiting you in the months and years that lie ahead. Pass every blessing on.

Love can and does go around the world. It is passed on the God-currents from one person to another.

When you spread a little sunshine in the heart of one person, that one is happy to pass it on and that's the way My life-giving, joy-giving message is spread.

Be transmitters these days. Love and laugh. Bring a smile to everyone. Love everyone.

Always seek to understand others and you cannot help but love them.

See Me in the simpleminded, the uninteresting, the sinful, the critical, the miserable.

See Me in the laughter of children and the sweetness of old age, in the courage of youth, and in the patience of adulthood.

ATTACK FEAR

Every day I teach the magnificent lesson of trusting Me and staying calm as you go through life's storms. Whatever sorrow or difficulty the day may bring, My tender command to you is still the same — *love and laugh*.

Love and laughter, not sorrowful resignation, are the signs of truly accepting My will. Let every person be braver and happier for having met you. *Love and laughter* should be your attitude towards children or youth, the middle-aged or elderly, for sorrow, for sin, for everything you may encounter in others.

Do not fear. Remember how I faced the devil in the wilderness (Matthew 4:1–11 NIV 1984), and how I conquered him with "the sword of the Spirit, which is the word of God" (Ephesians 6:17 ESV). You also must have your quick answer for every fear which evil may present — an answer of faith and confidence in Me. Whenever possible, say it out loud.

The spoken word has power. See every fear, not as a weakness on your part caused by illness or worry, but as a very real temptation to be attacked and overthrown.

THE SPIRIT OF A CHILD

Does the road seem to be rocky? Not one stone can slow your progress. Courage. Face the future, but *face* it only with a brave and happy heart. Do not try to *see* it. You are robbing faith of her magnificent sweetness if you try to see the future.

Just know that all is well and that faith, not seeing but believing (Hebrews 11:1), is the ferry that will carry you safely over the stormy waters. "According to your faith let it be done to you" (Matthew 9:29 NIV 2011) was My command to those who asked Me to heal them.

If faith was essential for working wonders, for healing and for salvation, it is clear why I insisted that everyone who wanted to enter My kingdom must become like little children (Matthew 18:3). Faith is the attitude of a child.

Seek in every way to become childlike. Seek, seek, seek until you find (Matthew 7:7). Seek until, over time, the nature of a trusting child becomes a part of you. You must copy the spirit of children not only for their simple trust, but for their joy in life, their ready laughter, their lack of criticism, their desire to share everything with everyone. Frequently ask to become like little children, friendly and loving toward everyone — not critical or fearful.

"Unless you change and become like little children, you will never enter into the kingdom of heaven" (Matthew 18:3b NIV 1984).

JULY 3
SPIRITUAL FULLNESS

Our Lord, we love You and desire to
live for You in all things.

My children, "You're blessed when you've worked up a good appetite for God. He's food and drink in the best meal you'll ever eat" (Matthew 5:6 MSG). Now *that* is satisfying.

Only in that fullness of spiritual things can the heartsick and weak and weary be satisfied, healed, and rested. We cry out, "Lord, to whom shall we go?" (John 6:68a NIV 1984). We proclaim, "You prepare a table before me" (Psalm 23:5a NIV 1984). Bread of Life — food from heaven.

How few people realize that the feeding of the four thousand (Matthew 15:32–38) and the five thousand (Matthew 14:13–21) were both illustrations of the way in which I would one day be the food for My people.

Just think of all the wonderful revelations that have yet to be seen by all those who live with Me. Although I lived on the earth hundreds of years ago, much of what I said and did is still a mystery; much of My life on earth is still spiritually unexplored territory. These things can only be revealed to those with simple and loving hearts who walk with Me. I have carefully "hidden these things from the wise and learned, and have revealed them to little children" (Luke 10:21 NIV 1984).

Do not weigh your spirits down with the sins and sorrows of the world. Only a Christ, a Messiah, can do that and live. Look for the loving, the true, the kind, the brave in all those around you.

JULY 4
FRIEND OF MINE

What people call conversion is often only the discovery of the Great Friend. What people call religion is the knowledge of the Great Friend. What people call holiness is the imitation of the Great Friend.

Perfection, the perfection I instructed you all to have, the being perfect as your Father in heaven is perfect (Matthew 5:48) is being like the Great Friend and, in turn, becoming a great friend to others, too.

I am your friend. Consider once again all that means — Friend *and* Savior. A friend is ready to help, anticipating every want. A friend waits with an outstretched hand to help and encourage, or to ward off danger. A friend's voice is one of tenderness to soothe tired nerves and speak peace to restlessness and fear.

Think of what your friend is to you. With that in mind, try to see a little of what the perfect Friend, the tireless, selfless, all-conquering, miracle-working Friend would be. *That* Friend, even more than your heart can imagine, I am that *Friend*.

If I were to take the doctrines of your churches and read them out loud to My kingdom — My kingdom of the childlike hearts — they would so often be met with resounding silence. But the simple rules I gave My followers are known, loved, and lived by them all.

In all things, seek simplicity.

JULY 5
YOU ARE INVINCIBLE

I am with you all the time — controlling, blessing, and helping you. No man or woman can thwart My will for you. A whole world of men and women cannot do this — if you trust Me and place your life in My hands.

It may seem to a passenger that each wave may capsize the ship or force it off course. The captain knows from experience that, in spite of winds and waves, he steers a course straight to the safe harbor he seeks.

So trust Me, the Captain of your salvation.

JULY 6
RICHES

Never let yourselves think, "We cannot afford this" or "We will never be able to do that." Say: "The means for it are not here yet, but will be supplied if we ought to have it. It *will* surely come."

Keep on saying that, and gradually a feeling of being abundantly supplied and of being surrounded by riches will come over you. That feeling is your faith claiming My supply, and "because of your faith, it will happen" (Matthew 9:29 NLT).

But it is not the faith expressed in moments of prayer and exultation I look for, but the faith that immediately lays to rest the doubts of the day as they arise, and attacks and conquers any sense of limitation.

"Ask, and you will receive" (John 16:24b ESV).

JULY 7
PAINFUL PREPARATION

Help and peace and joy are here. Your courage will be rewarded.

As painful as this time is, one day you will both see the reason why. You will realize that it was not cruel testing, but tender preparation for the extraordinary life-work you are both to do.

Try to realize that your own prayers are being answered most wonderfully. Answered in a way that seems painful to you, but that is the only way for now.

Success in the material world would not satisfy you.

Great success in both the material and the spiritual worlds awaits you.

I know you will see this had to be.

JULY 8
MY SECRET

You are being guided, but remember that I said, "I will guide you with My eye" (Psalm 32:8b NKJV).

And My eye is My resolute purpose — My will.

To guide with My will is to bring all your desires into oneness with My will, My desires.

Make My will your only will. Then My will guides you.

JULY 9
WHY DOUBT?

Rejoice in Me! Joy is infectious. Trust and pray. It is not a sin for someone who knows Me only as God, as Creator, to doubt Me, or to question My love and purposes.

But for someone who knows Me as you do, as Friend and Savior, and who knows the world's God as Father — for that one to doubt My purpose and saving power and tender love is wrong indeed.

JULY 10
EXPECT MANY MIRACLES

My provision for those I take care of is so wonderful.

Expect not one miracle, but many.

Everyday events, if caused and controlled by Me, are miracles.

JULY 11
GUARDIAN ANGELS

You are Mine. Once I have placed My stamp and seal of ownership on you, all of My angels gather to serve you and protect you.

Remember that you are daughters of a King.

Try to picture a bodyguard of My attendants in the unseen. They are waiting and longing to quickly do everything that is necessary for your well-being.

Feel this as you go through the day. Feel this, and all is well.

JULY 12
SAVIOR AND SAVIOR

If you believe that it is My hand that has saved you, then you must believe that I intend to continue saving you, and to keep you in the way that you should go.

Even a human rescuer does not save a drowning man only to place him in other deep and dangerous waters. To the contrary, he places him on dry land — and even more than that, there restores him to vitality and health, and then sees him to his home.

Let this parable teach you what I, your rescuer, would do and oh so much more. Is the Lord's arm too weak that it cannot perform and cannot save (Isaiah 59:1)?

My cry on the cross of "It is finished" (John 19:30a) is My cry of salvation for the whole world.

I complete every task entrusted to Me. So trust and do not be afraid.

JULY 13
EXPECT THE GOOD

Can you get an attitude of faith that expects the best?

Not waiting for the next bad thing to happen to you, but, with a child's joyful trust, awaiting the next good thing in store for you?

JULY 14
TRUE SUCCESS

Our Lord, we thank You
that You have kept us.

Rejoice indeed that you see My hand in everything which happened during the day, the things that changed as well as the things which stayed the same. Protected, the Israelites crossed the Red Sea (Exodus 13:17—14:31); likewise, you are protected in all things.

Rely on this truth and go forward. You have now entered the stage of success. You must not doubt this. You must see this. Beyond all doubt, you must know it. It is true. It is sure.

There is no age in eternal life. Reject self-pity. Have nothing but joy and gratitude.

These last few weeks, you have felt like the Israelites as they faced the Red Sea before they became aware of My rescue. Go forward now and conquer. Go forward unafraid!

JULY 15
SONGS ALONG THE WAY

Many of My disciples have had to stay in the dark, alone and friendless.

They struggled on, singing as they went.

For you, too, there must be songs along the way.

Would I plant your feet on an insecure ladder? You may not be able to see what the ladder rests on. Its supports may be hidden in the secret place of the Most High (Psalm 91:1 NKJV). But if I have asked you to step on and up firmly, then surely I have secured your ladder.

JULY 16
REFUGE

Know My divine power. Trust in Me. Dwell in My love. Laugh and trust. Laughter is a child's faith in God and goodness.

Seek safety in My secret place (Psalm 91).

You cannot be touched or harmed there. That is certain.

Genuinely feel as if you were in a strong tower (Psalm 61:3), heavily guarded, against which nothing can prevail.

JULY 17
PEACE, BE STILL

Rejoice, rejoice. I have so much to teach you both. Do not think that I am withholding My presence when I am not revealing more of My truth to you.

You are passing through a storm. It is enough that I am with you to say, "Peace, be still" (Mark 4:39 NKJV), to quiet both wind and waves.

It was on the quiet mountain slopes that I taught My disciples the truths of My kingdom (Matthew 5—7), not during the storm.

The same is true for you. The time of the mountain slopes will come, and you shall rest with Me and learn.

JULY 18
WALK HUMBLY

Fear of what others will say is a lack of trust in Me. This must not be. Convert all of these difficulties into the purification of your characters.

See yourselves as those around you see you, not as you wish to be, and "walk humbly with your God" (Micah 6:8b NIV 1984).

I will set you on high because you have known My name (Psalm 91:14), but it must be a purified you to be so exalted.

MARVELOUS HAPPENINGS

Our Lord, with hearts full of joy, we thank
You for Your marvelous blessings showered
upon us today and every day.

I am beside you. In all things, follow My guiding. There are marvels unfolding beyond your wildest imagination. I am your Guide. Rejoice in that thought. Your Guide and your Friend.

Remember that to Me, a miracle is only a natural happening. To My disciples, to My chosen, a miracle is only a natural happening. But it is a natural happening that operates through spiritual forces. Therefore, the man who works and understands only through the senses simply regards it as something contrary to nature.

Also remember that the "natural man" is at odds with God. Understand completely, and pray to understand more and more perfectly, that there is no wonder too marvelous to be an everyday happening for you, if you are guided and strengthened by Me.

My children, the children of My kingdom are My "own special people" (1 Peter 2:9 NKJV), set apart, with different hopes, aspirations, motives, and sense of reward.

You see a marvelous happening (like what happened today) occurring so easily, so simply, with no apparent cause, and you wonder.

Listen, My children, this has not happened easily and simply. It has been achieved by hours, days, and months of weariness and heartache battled against and overcome by a steadfast, unflinching desire to conquer "self," and to do My will and live out My teachings.

The concerns and the worries and the criticism patiently endured means spiritual power acquired, and operating marvelously.

JULY 20
MY STANDARDS

Carry out My commands, and leave the results to Me. Carry them out as obediently and faithfully as you would expect a child to solve a math problem using the rules he has been given. The child knows, without question, that if the rules are followed, the result will be correct.

Remember, the commands I have already worked out in the spirit world are the commands

I have given you in order to produce the required result in your specific case, based on your particular circumstances. So follow My rules faithfully.

Realize that the perfection of divine guidance lies in the fact that My commands are worked out to meet your exact circumstances. Following a man-made rule, even if it was laid down by the wisest person on earth, might lead to disaster.

Any person's knowledge of your life and character, capabilities, circumstances, and temptations must be incomplete to some extent. But to follow My direct guidance means to carry out the instructions given by the One who has full knowledge of both you and of the required result.

Each individual was meant to walk with Me in this way, to act under divine control, strengthened by divine power.

Haven't I taught you to love simplicity? No matter what the world may think, earth's goals and games are not for you. Oh! My children, learn from Me. Simplicity brings rest. True rest and power.

Simplicity may be foolishness to the world, but to Me, it is a foretaste of divinity. Never be led by the world's standards. Only *My* standards are for you.

JULY 21
THE WAY OF PRAISE

I am teaching you both My way of removing mountains. The way to remove mountains is the way of praise. When trouble comes, think of all you have to be thankful for. Praise, praise, praise.

Say, "Thank You" all the time. Your thankful hearts of praise are the removers of mountains.

JULY 22
MIRACLE OF THE AGES

L ive in me. Make your home in me just as I do in you" (John 15:4 MSG). "Anyone who believes in me will do the same works I have done, and even greater works, because I am going to be with the Father" (John 14:12 NLT).

"*Greater works!*" "The blind see, the lame walk, the lepers are cured, the deaf hear, the dead are raised to life, and the Good News is being preached to the poor" (Matthew 11:5 NLT). "And greater works than these he will do, because I go to My Father" (John 14:12b NKJV).

Wonder of the world! Miracle of the ages! God's power displayed in people who believe in Him! God's power going out to bless, by means of His people empowered by the Holy Spirit. Arise from the grave of sickness, poverty, doubt, sadness, limitation. "Arise, shine, for your light has come, and the glory of the Lord rises upon you" (Isaiah 60:1 NIV 1984).

A wonderful future is ahead for both of you. A future of unlimited power to bless others. Just be channels. Be used *by* Me and *for* Me. Ask. Ask. "If you remain in me and my words remain in you, you may ask for anything you want, and it will be granted!" (John 15:7b NLT). It will be granted to you and to those for whom you pray.

JULY 23
STOP ALL WORK UNTIL —

*Our Lord, grant us that
wonderful inner peace.*

My children, that peace truly does exceed anything we can understand (Philippians 4:7 NLT). No one can take that peace from you. No one has the power to disturb that peace, but you yourselves can let in the world, and its worries and distractions.

You can let in fears and sadness. You can open the door to the robber who breaks in on, and destroys, your peace.

Make it your responsibility to allow nothing to disturb your peace, the calmness of your heart, with Me. Stop all work, stop all dealings with others, until this is restored. Do not let those around you spoil your peace of heart and mind. Do not let anyone around you, any trouble, any irritation, or any problem disturb your peace for one moment.

Look at each difficulty as training to enable you to acquire this peace. Every task, every interruption — make up your mind that none of it can touch the harmony of the *real you* that is hidden with Me in the secret place of the Father (Psalm 91:1).

JULY 24
KEEP CLOSE

Our Lord, guide us. Show us Your will
and way in everything.

Keep close to Me, and you shall know the way, because, as I said to My disciples, "I am the way" (John 14:6). That is the solution to all of earth's problems.

Keep close, very close to Me. Think, act, and live in My presence.

How dare any enemy touch you, when you are protected by Me (Romans 8:31b)! That is the secret of all power, all peace, all purity, all persuasion: keeping very near to Me.

"Live in me. Make your home in me just as I do in you" (John 15:4a MSG). Live in My presence. Rejoice in My love. Thank Me and praise Me all the time. Wonders are unfolding.

JULY 25
WONDERFUL LIFE

I am your Lord. Lord of your lives, controller of your days, your present and your future. Leave all of your plans to Me. Only do what I tell you to do.

Both of you have now entered upon the God-guided life. Think about what that means. God-taught, God-guided.

Is anything too wonderful for such a life? Are you beginning to see how wonderful life with Me can be?

Do you see now that no evil can come against you?

JULY 26
FORGET — FORGIVE

Our Lord, we thank You for so much. We bless You and praise Your glorious name.

Fill your world with love and laughter. Never mind what heartache lies behind you.

Forget, forgive, love, and laugh.

Treat *everyone* as you would treat Me, with love and consideration.

Let nothing that others do to you change how you treat them.

JULY 27
MY CONSOLATION

Oh, Jesus, come and walk with us
and let us feel Your very nearness.

I walk with you. Just think, My children. I walk with you not only to guide and comfort you, and to strengthen and uphold you, but also for the comfort and consolation I Myself receive.

When a loving child is near you, is the only reason for him to be so close is that you may protect and help that little one?

Rather, you may find joy and delight in that little child, and comfort in his simplicity, love, and trust.

It is also in your power to comfort Me and bring joy to My heart.

JULY 28
MISTAKES

I am your shield. No attacks of the world can harm you. Feel as if there is a strong shield between you and all ridicule and humiliation. Practice feeling this until nothing has the power to spoil your inner peace. Then, indeed, a marvelous victory shall be won.

You sometimes wonder why you are permitted to make mistakes in your choices when you are really trying to do My will.

To that, I say it was no mistake ... Some of your lessons have to be learned the hard way, and your so-called mistake was needed to teach you a lesson. The promise is given, not to him who walks on with no obstacles in his way, but to him who overcomes (Revelation 3:21).

So in order to obtain peace quickly in your surroundings, as well as in your hearts, learn your lesson quickly. And the overcoming is never the overcoming of the person who troubled you, but the overcoming of weaknesses and wrongs in your own nature brought out by that person.

No lower standard than My standard shall be yours. "Be perfect, therefore, as your heavenly Father is perfect" (Matthew 5:48 NIV 1984).

SUNLIT CLEARINGS

Lord bless us in this evening hour,
and in Your mercy, heal us all.

Do not think that suffering is the only path into My kingdom. The steps and hearts of men are drawn to Me along sunlit clearings and paths surrounded by the loveliest of flowers. There are birds and laughter and butterflies and warm, life-giving summer air. With these as tender companions and friends, the way of joy into the kingdom can be taken.

Not all of the ways are bleak, cold, deserted, stony, and thorny. Leave everything to Me: the choice of the ways, and the guidance along the way. But when the sunlight calls, accept it gladly!

Even in the spiritual realm, appreciation comes from contrasting experiences. Who can better appreciate the warmth of the fireplace at home than the traveler who has just trudged through a blizzard? Take this cheerful message to heart: "He will not allow the temptation to be more than you can stand. When you are tempted, he will show you a way out so that you can endure" (1 Corinthians 10:13 NLT).

The world is not the kingdom. "In this world you will have trouble. But take heart! I have overcome the world" (John 16:33b NIV 1984). Live with Me, the conquering Christ, and the joy and peace of victory shall also be yours.

JULY 30
FAITH REWARDED

Think about the heroes of the faith often (Hebrews 11). How Abraham, even before he had a child, believed that all the nations on earth would be blessed through his descendants.

How Moses led the children of Israel through the desert, certain that at last the Promised Land would be theirs.

Down through the ages, there have always been those who obeyed, not seeing but believing (Hebrews 11:1), and their faith was rewarded. When you obey, believing but not seeing, your faith will be rewarded, too.

GRATITUDE

Give Me the gift of brave and thankful hearts.

A man proves his greatness by his power to see reasons to be thankful in his life.

When life seems hard, and troubles seem overwhelming, then you must definitely look for reasons to be thankful.

Your sacrifice, the offering of thanksgiving, is indeed a sweet incense going up to Me throughout your busy day.

Diligently search for something to be glad and thankful about in everything that happens, and soon no search will be required.

The reasons to be joyful and grateful will quickly become apparent to your loving hearts.

AUGUST 1
BLESSED BOND

Jesus, let Your beautiful presence
always be with us.

I will never fail you. I will never abandon you"
(Hebrews 13:5 NLT).

There is no connection in any earthly relationship that compares with the relationship between a soul who loves Me — and Me.

That friendship is more priceless than anyone on earth can imagine.

In the merging of heart and mind and will, a oneness results which only those who have experienced it can even begin to understand.

AUGUST 2
HARVEST

Our Lord, we seek Your blessing.

I love to pour My blessings down in rich and exquisite measure. But like sowing seeds, the ground must be prepared before the seed is dropped in.

Your job is to prepare the soil. My job is to drop the seed, the blessing, into the prepared soil.

Together we share and rejoice in the harvest.

Spend more time in preparing the soil. Prayer fertilizes soil. There is so much to do in preparation.

AUGUST 3
GIVE EVERY MOMENT TO ME

My children, how dear to My heart is the cry of love that asks for all of Me, that wishes every action, thought, word, and moment to be Mine.

It is a lack of understanding for someone to think that money given to this good cause or that is the great gift he has to offer. Above all else, I desire love — true, warm, childlike love — a trusting, understanding love. Next, the gift I most cherish is the gift of the moments, of *all* the moments.

I think even when love's impulsive desire to serve Me has offered Me all of life, every day, every hour, I think even then it is a long (and not easy) lesson, to learn what it means to give Me the moments.

The little things you planned to do which you give up gladly at My suggestion. The little acts of service done joyfully. See Me in everything, and then it will be easy to do.

This is a priceless time of initiation, but remember that the path of initiation is not for everyone. It is only for those who have felt the sorrowful cry of the world that needs a savior, and who have heard the tender plea of a Savior who desires followers through whom He can joyfully accomplish His great work of salvation.

AUGUST 4
ETERNAL LIFE

Oh, Jesus, we love You
and long to serve You.

My children, both of you are meant to do mighty things for Me. Glories and wonders are unfolding. Life is one glorious whole.

Take more and more of this wonderful eternal life into your beings. It is the flow of the eternal life through spirit, mind, and body that cleanses, heals, restores, renews youth, and passes on from you to others with the same miracle-working power.

"Now this is eternal life: that they may know you, the only true God, and Jesus Christ, whom you have sent" (John 17:3 NIV 1984). Therefore, seek to be in constant contact with Me in order to know Me more and more.

Make Me the one abiding presence during each day that you are aware of all the time. Seek to *do* less and to accomplish more, to achieve more. Doing is action. Achievement is successful action.

Remember that eternal life is the only lasting life, so that everything that is done without being done in the power of My Spirit, My life, passes away. Everything that is done in that Spirit-life is undying.

"And I give them eternal life, and they shall never perish; neither shall anyone snatch them out of My hand" (John 10:28 NKJV). So eternal life means security, too, safety. Live increasingly in the consciousness of that security, that safety.

AUGUST 5
HOUR OF NEED

Lord, come to us and heal us.

I am your healer, your joy, your Lord. You ask Me, your Lord, to come to you. Don't you know that I am already here? With silent footsteps, I draw near to you.

Your hour of need is the moment of My coming.

If you could know My love, if you could measure My longing to help, you would know that no agonized pleas are necessary.

Your *need* is what calls Me to you.

AUGUST 6
DWELL APART

Rest more with Me. If I, the Son of God, needed those times of quiet communion alone with My Father, away from noise, away from activity — then surely you need them, too.

Refilling with the Spirit is a need. That dwelling apart, that shutting yourself away in the very secret place of your being — away alone with Me.

From these times, you go forth in power to bless and to heal.

AUGUST 7
ALL IS WELL

Our Lord, bless us and keep us we beg You.

My power to keep you and protect you never fails. It is only your realization of it which fails. It is not a question of whether I can provide a shelter from the storm. The problem is your failure to be sure of the safety of that shelter.

Every fear, every doubt, is a crime against My love.

Oh, My children, trust Me! Every day, many times a day, practice saying, "All is well."

Say it until you believe it, until you *know* it.

AUGUST 8
EMPTY YOURSELF

Rely on Me alone. Ask for no other help. Surrender everything in the spirit of trust that more will come to supply your needs.

Empty your vessels quickly to ensure a divine supply.

The more that is retained by you, that much less will be gained from Me. It is a law of divine supply.

For you to hold things back, to keep them, implies a fear of the future, a lack of trust in Me.

When you ask Me to save you from the sea of poverty and difficulty, you must trust Me completely. If you do not trust Me completely, even though your prayer and faith are genuine, then I must first answer your prayer for help in the same way a rescuer approaches a drowning man who is struggling to save himself.

The rescuer renders him still more helpless and powerless until the man is wholly at the will and mercy of the rescuer. Understand that I can also lead you in this way. Trust Me wholly. Trust Me completely.

Empty your vessel. I will fill it. Both of you ask to understand divine supply. It is a very difficult lesson for My children to learn. They have become so dependent on material supply that they fail to understand. You must live as I tell you.

Depend on Me.

AUGUST 9
EFFORT AND REST

Come to Me, talk to Me, dwell with Me, and then you will know My way is a secure way, My paths are safe paths.

Come very close to Me.

Dig deep down into the soil of the kingdom. It is in the deep things of God where effort and rest meet.

AUGUST 10
STRAY SHEEP

Oh, Jesus, guide our footsteps
so we do not stray.

My children, there is no cure for straying except for keeping so close to Me that nothing — no interest, no temptation, no other person — can come between us.

Once you are certain of that truth, you have no choice but to stay at My side, knowing that because I am the very Way itself (John 14:6), nothing can prevent you from being in the Way, nothing can cause you to stray.

I have promised peace but not leisure, heart-rest and comfort but not pleasure. I have said, "Here on earth you will have many trials and sorrows" (John 16:33b NLT). When bad things happen, you should not feel as if you have failed or you are not being guided. But remember My *whole* statement was: "Here on earth you will have many trials and sorrows. *But take heart*, because I have overcome the world" (John 16:33b NLT, emphasis added).

So learn from Me the overcoming power of One who was spit on, scourged, misunderstood, forsaken, and crucified. Yet He could still see His work had not been affected by these things. He could still cry triumphantly from His cross, "It is finished" (John 19:30).

Finished. Not the pain, or the mocking, or the agony, but His task.

Let this thought comfort you. When you find yourself in the midst of failure, disharmony, abuse, and suffering, friends and angels may even now be preparing to sound the chorus of "It is finished!"

YOU ARE MINE

Jesus, You are watching over us to
bless us and to take care of us.

Yes! Always remember that. I am leading you out of darkness into light. Out of chaos to calm, out of disorder to order. Out of faults and failure to perfection.

So trust Me completely. Fear nothing. Always hope. Always look up to Me and I will be your "ever-present help" (Psalm 46:1 NIV 1984).

"I and My Father are one" (John 10:30 NKJV). He made the ordered, beautiful world out of chaos, and set the stars in the sky, and made each plant to know its season. Don't you think that He can also bring peace and order out of your little bit of chaos?

And He and I are One (John 10:30), and you are Mine (Isaiah 43:1b). Your affairs are Mine. It is My divine task to order My affairs — therefore, your affairs will be ordered by Me.

AUGUST 12
RULE THE WORLD

Remember that no prayer goes unanswered. Also remember, the very moment something seems wrong to you, or someone's actions do not seem to be what you think they should be, *that* is when your obligation begins to pray for those wrongs to be made right, or for that person to be different.

Face your responsibilities. What is wrong in your country, its leaders, its laws, its people? Quietly reflect on these questions, and make these concerns your prayer concerns. You will see lives changed you never touch, laws enacted at your request, evils banished.

Yes! Live without limits. Live to serve and to save. You may never even leave your room, and yet you may become one of the most powerful forces for good in your country, in the world.

You may never see the mighty work you do, but I see it, and the forces of evil see it. The life of one who saves is a glorious life indeed! You are co-laborers with Me. Realize this more and more.

Love with Me, you who share My life.

AUGUST 13
PERFECTION

Oh Jesus, help us, we beg You.

I am always your helper through dark to light, through weakness to power, through sin to salvation, through danger to security, through poverty to plenty, through indifference to love, through resentment to perfect forgiveness.

Never be satisfied by comparing yourself to those around you. Always bear in mind My clear instruction: "Be perfect, therefore, as your heavenly Father is perfect" (Matthew 5:48 NIV 1984). Do not settle for anything less.

Each of you must make it a habit to review your character. Consider how your character impacts all of your life: your loved ones, your household, friends, acquaintances, your country, your work.

See where I would act differently in the same relationships or circumstances or situations. Plan how to best eliminate a certain fault, or how to avoid a certain sin, mistake, or omission.

You must review your character at least once a week.

AUGUST 14
MY RICHEST GIFT

Jesus, you did come that we "may have and enjoy life, and have it in abundance (to the full, till it overflows)" (John 10:10b AMP).

Life, spiritual, mental, physical, abundant life—joyful life, powerful life. Yes, I came to give you these!

Don't you think My heart was sad because so few would accept that gracious gift?

Just think! The richest, most precious gift in the world being held out—free to everyone, and no one caring enough to stretch out a hand to take it.

Is that possible? My gift, the richest heaven has to offer, that precious gift of life, abundant life—man turns his back on, rejects, will have no part of.

Let this not be true of you. Take it quickly, and use it.

AUGUST 15
NOT PUNISHMENT

I will guide your efforts. You are not being punished for past sins. I have revealed My words to you from the very beginning. Now do what I told you to do. I have been showing you the way. You have not obeyed Me in this.

I have a plan that can only be revealed through your obedience. I rarely find two souls who are united in wanting only to do My will, and only to serve Me. That union is miracle-working.

I have told you that I am longing to use you. All nations would have been made disciples (Matthew 28:19–20) long ago if I had been served by many such "two souls."

It was always "two by two" (Luke 10:1).

AUGUST 16
NO TIRED WORK

Rest. It is wrong to work as if you were being forced to do it. Rest until life, eternal life, flowing through your veins and hearts and minds, inspires you to get started. Then work, glad work, will follow.

Tired work is never effective.

Rest. Remember, I am your physician, the healer of mind and body.

Look to Me for healing, for rest, for peace.

AUGUST 17
NATURE LAUGHS

I come, I come. You need Me. Spend a lot of time outside.

My sunshine, My glorious air, My presence, My teaching. Wouldn't they make a vacation spot for you anywhere? Sunshine gladdens a man's heart. It is the laughter of nature.

Spend a lot of time outside. My medicines are sun and air, trust and faith. Trust is the sunshine of the spirit, your entire being wrapped up in the divine Spirit.

Faith is the soul's breathing in of the divine Spirit. Mind, soul, and body need helping. Welcome My tender care for you both. Draw near to Me.

Nature is often My nurse for tired souls and weary bodies. Let her have her way with you both.

STONES ALONG THE WAY

I am here. No distance keeps Me from you. In My kingdom, the spiritual kingdom, we do not measure in miles like you do on earth. A false word, a fear-inspired failure, a harsh criticism, these are the things that create a distance between a soul and Me. Your training must be severe so that nothing interferes with your work for Me.

You seek My presence, and they who seek shall find (Jeremiah 29:13). It is not a question of a man searching for My presence, so much as his being aware of My presence. Unconditional surrender to My will, in the small as well as the big things of life, is what makes My guidance possible.

You know the difference between taking along a happy, loving child bouncing with joy, who anticipates each instruction, accepts your guidance naturally at each turn — as opposed to the child who resists, rebels, and has to be forced, even though in his quieter moments he may say, "Yes. I do want to go with you. I cannot be left alone, but I hate this way."

What matters with My disciples is not the path, but the loving rejoicing in the way and in My guidance. You are both ready for the guidance, but neither of you rejoices as you should in the little, daily stones along the way (James 1:2).

AUGUST 19
A HUMAN TEMPLE

Lord, we love You. We worship You.

Bow low before Me. Worship is not prayer, although both express different ways people need Me. Bow low in worship, aware not only of My humanity but also of My divine majesty.

As you kneel in humble adoration, I will tell you that when I took your humanity upon Me, it was with the desire of raising that humanity to My divinity.

Earth gave Me her best—a human temple to contain My divinity. And I brought to her the possession of divine power, divine love, and divine strength to be forever expressed in those of her children who accepted Me, opened their hearts to Me, and attempted to live My life.

So, kneeling in a spirit of humility, turn your eyes heavenward and realize the majesty, the power, and the beauty that may be yours. Remember, there are no limits to My giving — even though there may be limits to your accepting.

Oh! Rejoice at the wonders to which you are called and, seeing them in prayer, rise in My strength, filled with the longing to attain them.

AUGUST 20
SHAME AND REMORSE

My children. Yes! I am the shield from contempt and the cover from disapproval. Frequently, I have to shield My disciples from their contempt and disapproval of themselves.

My poor disciple Peter could never have done My work, could never have had the courage to live on, or the daring to live for Me without his being wrapped in My tender love. I did not need to protect him from the anger of My Father, who is all love — nor from the scorn of My enemies, nor from the resentment of My friends. No! I needed to protect Peter from hating himself.

Today, as before, My followers experience the shame and remorse and contempt of themselves, of their weak selves. They meant to be so strong and brave for Me. And then I have to protect them with a shield of love or they could never have the courage to fight and conquer. But this facing of the real self has to be — shame and remorse must come.

That is a stage of development, but *only* a stage. What use would the beautiful wings of a butterfly be if it remained earthbound, weighed down by the memory of its pitiful past as a caterpillar? And so now, this very day, I tell you both that you must not dwell, even for one moment, on your sins and mistakes and faults and bad habits of the past.

You must be like a man who runs a race, stumbles and falls, but then rises and presses on to the goal. What good would it do if he stayed to examine the spot where he fell, to weep over the delay, over the shortsightedness that prevented his anticipating and avoiding the obstacle?

It is the same with you, and I give it to you as a command — no looking back. Give yourself and everyone you have ever met a fresh start from today. Don't remember their sins or failures, or your own.

The remembrance is a current of disappointment that slows down the swimmer.

When I sent My disciples out two by two — no baggage, no extra coat, no money (see Matthew 10:9–10) — it was a command to be carried out literally, but figuratively as well. On life's journey, throw away all that is not important. Cast aside all the obstacles, the past imperfections of others, the sense of failure.

Travel unburdened, with a light heart. And the lighter your heart, the greater weight of influence you will have.

My children, I love you.

AUGUST 21
BROKEN VOICES

Behold, I make all things new" (Revelation 21:5 NKJV). It is only the earthbound spirit that cannot soar. Every blessing I send you, every joy, every freedom achieved from poverty and worry will loosen a strand that ties you to earth.

It is only those strands that bind you. Therefore, your freedom will mean your rising into the realm of joy and appreciation.

Clipped wings can grow again. Broken voices regain a strength and beauty unknown before. Soon, you will delight in your power to help others when it seemed too late for you to receive any help that would bring you joy.

Worn-out, pain-weary, and tired as you may seem, I say to you, "Behold, I make all things new." That promise shall be fulfilled. My loved ones, I speak to you tenderly across the years. Yet I also speak today tenderly close and near to your tired ears, worn out by the deafening noise.

"Come to me, all of you who are weary and carry heavy burdens, and I will give you rest" (Matthew 11:28 NLT).

AUGUST 22
GLEAMS OF SUNLIGHT

Because you have both longed to save My world, I let you have the training which will equip you to save.

Each day, both of you are to take your pains and sufferings, difficulties and hardships, and offer them up for one troubled soul, or for some prayer which especially needs to be answered.

So the beauty of each day will live on after the day's trouble, distress, difficulty, and pain have passed.

From My life, learn about the suffering that saves others. Then you will sing in your pain. There are gleams of sunlight across the grayest of days.

AUGUST 23
THE SUMMIT

Do not see the small trials and irritations in each hour of every day. See the one purpose and plan to which everything is leading. If while climbing a mountain, you keep your eyes on each rocky or difficult place as you ascend, seeing nothing but that, how exhausting and pointless your climb!

But if you think of each step as leading to the summit of achievement, from which glories and beauties will open out before you, then your climb will be oh so different.

AUGUST 24
MAGNIFICENT HEIGHTS

Our Lord, we know that You are
great and able to deliver us.

I am your deliverer. Trust in Me absolutely. Know that I will do the very best for you. Be ready and willing for My will to be done.

Know that with Me, all things are possible (Matthew 19:26b). Cling joyfully to that truth.

Say many times, "All things are possible with my Master, my Lord, my Friend."

This truth, accepted and firmly believed in, is the ladder up which a soul can climb from the lowest of pits to the most magnificent of heights.

AUGUST 25
EXHAUSTION

We seek You as You have told us.

And seeking, you shall find (Jeremiah 29:13). No one ever sought My presence in vain. No one ever sought My help in vain.

At a mere whisper of desire for Me, My Spirit is there—to replenish and renew. Sometimes weariness and exhaustion are not signs of a lack of spirit, but of the guiding of the Holy Spirit.

Many wonderful things would not have happened without the physical weariness, the mind-weariness of My servants, which necessitated the resting apart with Me, the giving up of work.

Although My way may seem to be a narrow way (Matthew 7:13–14), nevertheless, it leads to life, abundant life (John 10:10b). Follow it. It is not too narrow for Me to walk beside you.

You will never be too lonely with such companionship. A Friend infinitely tender, infinitely strong, will walk the way with you.

AUGUST 26
ACCEPT TRIALS

Troubles and trials may seem to overwhelm you. But all they can do is accomplish My will, and you have said My will is your will.

Don't you see that you cannot be destroyed?

From now on, a new life is opening up before you. It is time for you to enter into the kingdom I have prepared for you (Matthew 25:34).

The sunlight of My presence is on your paths. Trust and go forward unafraid. My grace is sufficient for all your needs. (2 Corinthians 12:9).

AUGUST 27
CHAOS

"Your strength will come from settling down in complete dependence on me ..."
(ISAIAH 30:15 MSG)

Feel that ... Trust Me. Aren't I leading you safely, faithfully? Will you believe Me, your Master, that all of this is really meant to bring the answers to your prayers?

Remember that I am the Supreme Being who knows everything and can control everything. As soon as you put your affairs, their confusion and their difficulties, into My hands, I immediately begin to effect a cure for all of the conflict and chaos.

You must know that My cure will cause you no more pain than a doctor, who makes plans knowing that he can effect a cure, would cause his patient. I will do everything as tenderly as possible.

Tell Me that you trust Me in this.

AUGUST 28
CONTINUOUS SERVICE

Service is the law of heaven. My angels always obey. "They serve Him continually" can be said about them — and everyone who loves Me.

With love, there is continuous service, service in every action done for Me, as well as in resting in Me.

Take this not as the end but as the beginning of a new life devoted to My service.

A life of power and joy.

AUGUST 29
BREATHE MY NAME

Just breathe My name.

It is like the squeeze of a child's hand that brings a responsive squeeze, strengthens the child's confidence, and banishes fear.

AUGUST 30
GIVE, GIVE, GIVE

Give abundantly. Feel like you are rich. Have no stingy thought in your heart.

Give, give, give: of love, of thought, of everything you have.

You are followers of the world's greatest Giver. Give of your time, of personal ease and comfort, of rest, of fame, of healing, of power, of sympathy — of all these and many more.

Learn this lesson, and you will become a great power to help others, and to do mighty things.

AUGUST 31
PRAY AND DENY

"This kind can come out by nothing
but prayer and fasting."
(MARK 9:29 NKJV)

You must live a life of fellowship and prayer if you are to save others.

Take My words as a command to you. "By prayer and fasting."

Pray and deny yourself, and you will be used marvelously to help and save others.

SEPTEMBER 1
HOW RICH YOU ARE

"I will never fail you.
I will never abandon you."
(HEBREWS 13:5 NLT)

My children, that promise is unfailingly true. Down through the centuries, thousands have proven My dependability, My endurance, My unfailing love. "Never fail." "Never abandon." It does not simply mean that My presence will be with you, but so much more.

My love will never leave you, My understanding will never leave you, My strength will never leave you.

Think of all that I am:

Love — then forever you are sure of love.

Strength — then forever, in every difficulty and danger, you are sure of strength.

Patience — then there is always One who can never grow weary.

Understanding — then you will always be understood.

Can you fear the future when it holds so much for you? Beloved, "set your mind on things above" (the higher, spiritual things) and "not on things on the earth" (the lower, material things) (Colossians 3:2 NKJV), and you will see how rich you are.

SEPTEMBER 2
I MUST PROVIDE

I am your Lord. Enough. Then I can command your obedient service, your loyalty. But as your Lord, I am also required to protect you.

I am required to fight for you, to plan for you, to meet your every need with all that is within My power to provide. Think how vast that provision can be. Never doubt.

Such marvels are unfolding. Wonders beyond your dreams. They only need the watering of a grateful spirit and a loving heart to bring an abundant harvest.

SEPTEMBER 3
LIVE IN THE UNSEEN

Our Lord, the God of the troubled
and the weary, come and save us.

I am your Savior. Not only from the weight of sin, but from the weight of worry, from misery and depression, from poverty and problems, from weakness and heartache. Your Savior.

Remember that you are really living in the unseen — that is the real life.

Lift up your heads from earth's troubles, and view the glories of the kingdom. Look higher and higher each day and see more of heaven. Speak to Me. Long for Me. Rest in Me. Remain in Me (John 15:4–7). Do not restlessly bring Me your burdens, and then frantically pick them back up and carry them away.

No! Remain in Me. Do not lose the consciousness of My strength and protection for even a moment.

Like a child in her mother's arms, stay safe and at rest.

SEPTEMBER 4
DROP THOSE BURDENS

Our God is our supply.

Look to Me for everything … Rely on Me for everything. Drop those burdens and then, singing and free, you can go on your way rejoicing. Burdened with them, you will fall.

Drop them at My feet, knowing beyond any doubt that I will pick them up and deal with each one as is truly best.

SEPTEMBER 5
PROGRESS

Progress is the law of heaven. Higher, ever higher, rise to life and beauty, knowledge and power. Higher and higher.

Tomorrow, be stronger, braver, and more loving than you have been today.

The law of progress gives meaning to life, a purpose to life.

SEPTEMBER 6
YOUR LOVED ONES

Your loved ones are very safe in My keeping. Learning and loving and working, theirs is a life of happiness and progress. They live to serve, and they truly do serve. They serve Me and those they love. They serve without ceasing.

But their acts of service are so numerous and so varied, you can no more see them than the people around Me could see the angels who ministered to Me in the wilderness (Mark 1:13b).

People so often rush to earthly friends who can serve them in so limited a way. Your loved ones who have gone to heaven before you are friends who are freed from the limitations of humanity.

Such friends can serve you so much better, understand better, protect better, plan better, and even plead your cause with Me better.

It is good for you to remember your friends in heaven. The more time you spend with them, the more you live in this unseen world, the gentler your own passing will be when it comes. Even now, troubles and difficulties on earth will seem less overwhelming as you look, not at the things that are seen, but at the real, the eternal life.

"Now this is eternal life: that they may know you, the only true God, and Jesus Christ, whom you have sent" (John 17:3 NIV 1984).

Learning to know Me draws that kingdom very near, and in Me, and through knowledge of Me, the dear ones there become *very* near and dear.

SEPTEMBER 7
EVERLASTING ARMS

"The eternal God is your refuge, and
underneath are the everlasting arms."
(DEUTERONOMY 33:27 NIV 1984)

Arms, sheltering arms, express the loving tenderness of your Father, My Father, in heaven. In their trouble and difficulty, what people need more than anything else is a refuge. A place in which to hide. A place where no one and nothing can touch them.

Say to yourself, "He is our refuge." Say it until its truth sinks into your very soul. Say it until you know it — are so sure of it — that nothing can make you afraid.

Feel this until fear flees, and keep on feeling it until joy ripples through in its place. Refuge. Everlasting arms, so untiring, so safe — so sure.

SEPTEMBER 8
WALK IN MY LOVE

When supply seems to have run out, you must know that is not true. It is then you must look around to see what you can give away. Give away something.

When supply seems short, things are stagnating, being blocked. Your giving clears that away and lets the spirit of My supply flow freely.

Knowing that I am present and that I am love makes all of life different. Your consciousness of Me means the opening of your whole nature to Me, and that brings relief. Relief brings peace. Peace brings joy. A "peace which is too wonderful to understand" (Philippians 4:7 WE) and the "joy no one will take from you" (John 16:22 NKJV).

My love and care for you are greater than words can describe. Be certain of that. Rejoice in it. *Walk in My love.* These words mean so much. There is a joy, a spring, a gladness in the walk of those who walk in My love. That walk becomes a glad, conquering, and triumphant march. So walk.

SEPTEMBER 9
CULTIVATE YOURSELF

In Your strength, we conquer.

Yes! You gain your conquering power from Me. There can be no failure with Me. Therefore, the secret of success is life with Me.

Do you want to make the most of life? Then live very near to Me, the Master and Giver of all life. Your reward is guaranteed. It will be perfect success, but it will be *My* success.

Sometimes the success of souls won, sometimes the success of diseases cured or demons cast out. Sometimes the success of a finished sacrifice like that on Calvary. Sometimes the success of one who never said a word in response to the ridicule and torture and mocking cries of His enemies, or the success of a risen Savior as He walked through the garden of Joseph of Arimathea on that first Easter morning.

But *My* success. The world may consider you to be failures. The world does not judge the way I judge.

Kneel before Me in wonder of My revelation. The joy of seeing spiritual truths is a great joy. When the heavens are opened and the voice speaks, it will not be to all hearts, but only to the faithful, loving hearts.

Remember your largest field of labor is yourself. That is your first task: the weeding, planting, digging, pruning, and ultimately, the bearing of fruit. When that is done, I will lead you out into other fields.

SEPTEMBER 10
GOD OR MONEY?

You must be ready to take a stand that is different from that of the world. Do you want the full and complete satisfaction that you find in Me, as well as the satisfaction that the world offers? Then you are trying to serve God and money (Matthew 6:24), or if not trying to serve both, then claiming the benefits of both God and money.

If you work for Me, you will have your reward. But then you turn to the world, to human beings, and expect that reward, too. This is not right.

Do not expect love or gratitude or acknowledgement from anyone else. I will give you all the reward that is necessary.

SEPTEMBER 11
A GENEROUS GIVER

"I have come that they may have life, and
that they may have it more abundantly."
(JOHN 10:10 NKJV)

Yes, I, your Master, am a generous giver. I give to you abundant life, in overflowing measure. That is the reason I came, to give life to souls. The life, eternal life, that pulses through your whole being, that animates both your mind and your body.

A generous giver. A kingly giver. I came so that men might live in Me. It was this life I was talking about when I said, "I am the vine; you are the branches" (John 15:5 NIV 1984). The life flow of the vine is also in the branches.

Our lives are one — yours and Mine. All that is in My nature must therefore flow into yours, when we are so closely connected.

I am love and joy and peace and strength and power and healing and humility and patience, and everything else you see in Me, your Lord. Then you must also have these as My life flows through you. So have courage.

You do not make yourselves loving and strong and patient and humble. You live with Me, and then My life accomplishes those miraculous changes in you.

SEPTEMBER 12
THE VALUE OF MONEY

*"But seek first the kingdom of God
and His righteousness, and all these
things shall be added to you."*
(MATTHEW 6:33 NKJV)

*"If therefore thine eye be single, thy
whole body shall be full of light."*
(MATTHEW 6:22B KJV)

The eye of the soul is the will. If your one desire is My kingdom, to find that kingdom, to serve that kingdom, then truly, your whole body shall be full of light.

When you are told to seek first the kingdom of God, the first step is to make sure that your will is for that kingdom. A single eye to God's glory. Desiring nothing less than that His kingdom come. Seeking the advancement of His kingdom in all things.

Have no values but spiritual values. No profit except that of spiritual gain. Seek His kingdom first in all things.

Only seek material gain when it means a gain for My kingdom. Completely reject using money as a measure of worth. Walk with Me. Learn about Me. Talk to Me. This is where your true happiness lies.

SEPTEMBER 13
NO OTHER NAME

My name is the power that banishes evil and commands all good to help you. Evil spirits flee at the sound of "Jesus." Spoken in fear, in weakness, in sorrow, or in pain, it is a request for help I will always answer. "Jesus."

Use My name often. Think about how a mother's children are constantly calling out, "Mom!" To help, to care, to decide, to appeal, "Mom." Use My name in that same way — simply, naturally, forcefully. "Jesus."

Use it not only when you need help, but to express love. Spoken out loud, or in the silence of your hearts, it will change an atmosphere from one of tension to one of love. It will raise the standard of conversation and thought. "Jesus."

"There is no other name under heaven given to men by which we must be saved" (Acts 4:12 NIV 1984).

SEPTEMBER 14
WHEN FAITH FAILS

"Lord I believe; help my unbelief!"
(MARK 9:24 NKJV)

This cry of the human heart is still as expressive of human need as it was when spoken to Me while I was on earth. It expresses the soul's progress.

As a soul understands Me and My power, and knows Me as Helper and Savior, that soul believes in Me more and more. At the same time, it is more conscious than before of its falling short of absolute trust in Me.

"Lord, I believe; help my unbelief!" The soul's progress is increased belief. Then comes a cry for still more faith — a plea to conquer all unbelief, all lack of trust.

That cry is heard. That prayer is answered. More faith, and at the same time, more power to see where trust is lacking.

My children, seek to go up this path, with each step leading closer to Me.

SEPTEMBER 15
QUIET STRENGTH

Rest in Me. When you are exhausted, it is a call for you to rest. Then rest until My life-power flows through you.

Have no fear of the future. Be quiet. Be still. And in that stillness your strength will come and will be maintained.

The world equates strength with "doing." In My kingdom, it is known that strength lies in quiet. "In quietness and trust is your strength" (Isaiah 30:15 NIV 1984).

What a promise! What glorious fulfillment! The strength of peace and the peace of strength. Rest in Me. Rejoice in Me.

SEPTEMBER 16
ASSURANCE

"The work of righteousness will be peace, and the effect of righteousness, quietness and assurance forever."
(ISAIAH 32:17 NKJV)

It is My peace which gives quietness and assurance forever. My peace that flows like a calm river through the dry land of life. That causes the trees and flowers of life to bloom and to bring forth an abundant harvest.

Success is the result of work done in peace. It is only in this way that work can produce its results. Don't over-schedule. You do not live in time, but in eternity. Your future is being planned in the unseen.

Abide in Me, and I in you, and you will bear much fruit (John 15:5). Be calm, assured, at rest. Love, not hurry. Peace, not worry. Nothing restless. All successful. Sown in prayer, watered by trust, bearing flower and fruit in joy. I love you.

SEPTEMBER 17
STUMBLING STEPS

*Show us Your way, O LORD, and let us
walk in Your paths (see Psalm 25:4).*

You are walking in My paths. This is the way. The way of an uncertain future and stumbling steps. It is My way ...

Put aside all fear of the future. *Know* that you will be led. *Know* that you will be shown the way. I have promised.

DWELL THERE

"He who dwells in the secret place
of the Most High shall abide under
the shadow of the Almighty."
(PSALM 91:1 NKJV)

Hidden in a secure place, known only to God and you. So secret that no power on earth can even find it.

But, My beloved children, you must *dwell* there. Not occasional visits, but a real abiding. Make it your home. Your dwelling place.

My shadow shall rest over that home to make it doubly safe, doubly secret. My shadow rests like the wings of a mother bird protecting her young. How safe, how secure, you must feel there.

When fears attack you and worries weigh you down, it is because you have ventured out of that protective shadow. Then the one, the *only*, thing to do is to make your way back into the shelter again. So rest.

SEPTEMBER 19
FULL JOY

"I have told you these things so
that you will be filled with my joy.
Yes, your joy will overflow!"
(JOHN 15:11 NLT)

Remember, the truths that I taught My disciples which I am now teaching you have been given for the same purpose: to give you that overflowing joy.

Search for the joy in life. Hunt for it like you would seek hidden treasure. Love and laugh. *Delight* yourselves in the Lord (Psalm 37:4).

Rejoice in Me. My wish was for My disciples to have full joy. I intended for them to have it. If they had lived out My teachings in their daily lives, they would have had fullness of joy.

SEPTEMBER 20
TASTE AND TRUST

"Taste and see that the LORD is good."
(PSALM 34:8 NIV 1984)

He is good. Trust in Him. Know that all is well. Say "God is good. God is good." Just leave the present and the future in His hands. The only thing you need to know is that God is good. He can bring order out of chaos, good out of evil, peace out of turmoil. God is good.

"I and My Father are one" (John 10:30 NKJV). One in desire to do good. For God to do good to His children is for Him to share His goodness with them. God is good, eager to share His goodness and good things with you, and He *will* do this.

Trust and do not be afraid (Isaiah 12:2 NIV 1984).

SEPTEMBER 21
SEE THE FATHER

"Lord, show us the Father,
and it is sufficient for us."
(JOHN 14:8 NKJV)

My children, I have been with you so long, spending time with you and speaking to you. How can it be that you have not known the Father?

Your Father is the God and Controller of a mighty universe. But He is the same as I am (John 10:30). All the love and the strength and the beauty you have seen in Me are in My Father.

If you see that, and know Him and Me as we really are, then that is sufficient for you — is truly enough for you — completes your life — satisfies you — is all you need.

See the Father, see Me, and it is sufficient for you. This is love in abundance. Joy in abundance. All you need.

SEPTEMBER 22
JOYFUL TRIBUTE

Jesus, our Lord, we adore You.

Sing to Me from a glad heart. Sing and praise My holy name. Praise is man's joyful tribute to Me. As you praise, thrills of joy surge through your being, and you get a taste of the joy known by the heavenly host.

SEPTEMBER 23
TURN AGAIN

"Draw near to God and He will draw near to you."
(JAMES 4:8 NKJV)

This is a law in the spiritual life. You must turn to Me before you are conscious of My being near you. You must learn to turn to Me in every circumstance, whether it is gladly turning to Me with thanksgiving, or humbly turning to Me to whisper your request.

It is so wonderful that nothing is needed except that silent appeal. You do not need to give voice to your longing. No need to beg, no need to bring gifts. How wonderful to feel you can so simply claim help, and it is there so promptly, so lovingly.

Not only help, but the comfort and joy of divine nearness and companionship. A nearness that brings sweetness, confidence, and peace into your life.

Never fear, never lose heart. Draw near to Me, and all you need is in that nearness. Just My presence alone can transform conditions and lives — bring harmony and beauty, peace and love.

SEPTEMBER 24
LEARN FROM ME

"Master, to whom would we go? You have the words of real life, eternal life."
(JOHN 6:68, MSG)

Learn from no one except Me. Teachers are supposed to point the way to Me. After that, you must accept Me, the Great Teacher.

The words of eternal life are all the words controlling your whole being, even controlling your earthly life. Take these from Me also. Have no fear. Abide in Me and accept My being the Lord of your life.

Be full of gratitude. Send your prayers to heaven on the wings of praise. Accept everything that happens as having been planned by Me. All is well. I have prepared everything out of My love for you. Let your heart sing.

SEPTEMBER 25
COME AND STAY

"Come to me, all you who are weary and
burdened, and I will give you rest."
(MATTHEW 11:28 NIV 1984)

Yes, come for rest. But stay for rest, too. Stop all frantic rushing around, and be calm and untroubled. Come to Me, not only for your prayers to be answered, but to be close to Me.

Be certain of My help, be aware of My presence, and wait until My rest fills your soul.

Rest knows no fear. Rest knows no want. Rest is strong, certain. The rest of soft meadows and peacefully flowing rivers, of strong immovable hills. Rest, and all you need to attain this rest is to come to Me. So come.

SEPTEMBER 26
SERVE EVERYONE

"I am among you as one who serves."
(LUKE 22:27 NIV 1984)

Yes! Remember to serve everyone. Be ready to prove you are My child by serving. Regard everyone you meet as guests in your Father's house, to be treated with love, with every consideration, with gentleness.

As a servant of everyone, do not consider any work to be beneath you. Always be ready to do everything you can for others. Serve. Serve. Serve.

There is a gladness in service, a joy in doing My will for others, in being My expression of everything that is good for them.

Remember, when you serve others, you are acting on behalf of your Master and Lord who washed His disciples' feet. So, in serving others, express your love for Me.

SEPTEMBER 27
DIVINE RESTRAINT

Is My hand shortened that it cannot save (Isaiah 59:1)? No! My power to save increases as your power to understand My salvation increases. So from strength to strength, from power to power, we go forward united.

There is no limit to My power to work miracles in the universe. There are, however, limitations to My miracle-working power in the lives of individuals, but only to the extent that person lacks vision. There is no limit to My power to save. Also, there is no limit to My desire and longing to save. My hand is not shortened, and it is still outstretched, longing and waiting to be allowed to bless and help and save.

Think how tenderly I respect the right of each individual soul. I never force anyone to accept My help, My salvation. Perhaps in all My suffering for humanity, this is the most difficult: the restraint of My divine impatience and desire to help, until the cry of the soul gives Me permission to act.

Think of My love shown in this. My waiting, loving, longing heart is comforted when you claim My help, guidance, and miracle-working power.

SEPTEMBER 28
THE SECRET PATH

*"Let it be so now; it is proper for us
to do this to fulfill all righteousness."*
(MATTHEW 3:15 NIV 1984)

My three years' mission on earth was founded on accepting the difficulty and discipline of life in order to share the human experience with My followers throughout the ages.

Much of what you both must accept in life is not to be accepted as being necessary for you personally. Rather, you must accept it, as I accepted it, to set an example, to share in the sufferings and difficulties of mankind.

In this context, "to share" means "to save." In this, the same must be true for the both of you as it was so true of Me. "He saved others, but he can't save himself" (Matthew 27:42 NIV 1984).

Beloved, you are called to save and share in a very special way. The way of sorrows, if walked with Me, the Man of Sorrows (Isaiah 53:3), is a path kept sacred and secret for My nearest and dearest: for those whose one desire is to do everything for Me, to sacrifice everything for Me, to consider as My servant Paul did, everything as a loss so that others might gain Me (Philippians 3:8).

But, as dreary as that path must look to those who only view it from afar, it has tender lights and restful shades that no other walk in life can offer.

SEPTEMBER 29
I TOUCH YOUR ARM

"Thy touch has still its ancient power."
("AT EVEN, ERE THE SUN WAS SET,"
HENRY TWELLS, 1868)

Yes! When you are quiet before Me, I lay My hand upon each head, and My divine Spirit flows through that healing, powerful touch into your very beings. Wait in silence before Me until you feel that.

When you look to Me for guidance, My hand is placed upon your arm, a gentle touch to point the way. When you cry out to Me for healing of mind, body, or spirit, My touch brings strength and healing, the renewal of your youth, and the power to climb and strive.

When you become exhausted along the way, and your stumbling footsteps show human strength is failing, the touch of My strong and helping hand supports you on your way.

Yes! My children, My touch still has its ancient power, and that power is promised to you. So go forward into the future bravely and unafraid.

SEPTEMBER 30
WISDOM

"As your days, so shall your strength be."
(DEUTERONOMY 33:25 NKJV)

I have promised that for every day you live, the strength shall be given to you. Do not fear.

Face each difficulty being certain that the wisdom and strength for it will be given to you. Claim it.

Rely on Me to keep My promise about this. In My universe, for every task I give one of My children, all that is necessary to perform it has already been set aside. So why fear? So why doubt?

SECRET OF PROSPERITY

"Let all the world look to me for salvation!"
(ISAIAH 45:22 NLT)

Do not look to any other source for salvation. Look only to Me. Look for no other supply. Look to Me, and you shall be saved. Regard Me as your only supply. That is the secret of prosperity for you. And you, in turn, shall save many others from poverty and adversity.

Whatever danger threatens, look to Me. Whatever you desire or need, or desire or need for others, look to Me. Claim it all from My storehouse. Claim, claim, claim.

Remember that I fed the children of Israel with heaven-sent manna (Exodus 16). I made a way through the Red Sea for them (Exodus 14:10–31). I led them through the wilderness of destitution, difficulty, and discipline. I led them into Canaan, "a land flowing with milk and honey" (Exodus 3:8). So trust. So be led.

Rejoice. These are your wilderness days. But surely and safely, you are being led to your Canaan of plenty.

OCTOBER 2
TRUE MEEKNESS

How easy it is for Me to lead and guide you when you are responsive to My wishes! The hurts of life only come when you, or your loved ones, try to go your own way and resist the pressure of My hand.

There must be a gladness in choosing My will. Delight to do that will.

I said the meek shall inherit the earth (Matthew 5:5). That is, they shall control others and the material resources of the earth.

But this exalted position of stewardship is the result of a yielded will. That was My meaning of the word "meek."

So live. So yield. So conquer.

OCTOBER 3
BLESSED ASSURANCE

"The work of righteousness will be peace, and the effect of righteousness, quietness and assurance forever."
(ISAIAH 32:17 NKJV)

Be still, and know that I am God" (Psalm 46:10 NIV 1984). It is only when the soul achieves this calm that true work can be done. Only then will mind and soul and body be strong to conquer and endure.

Peace is the work of righteousness (being in right standing with Me) — living the right life, living with Me. Quietness and assurance follow.

Assurance is the calm born of a deep certainty in Me, in My promises, in My power to save and keep. Obtain this calm, and at all costs, keep this calm. Rest in Me. Live in Me. Calm, quiet, assured — at peace.

OCTOBER 4
ALL YOU DESIRE

"He had no beauty or majesty to attract us to him, nothing in his appearance that we should desire him."
(ISAIAH 53:2B NIV 1984)

My children, in this verse, My servant Isaiah spoke of the wonderful revelation given to those who were guided by My Spirit.

To those who don't know Me, there is nothing in Me to appeal to them or to attract them.

To those who do know Me, there is nothing more desirable even though there is "nothing in his appearance that we should desire him."

Oh! My children, draw very near to Me. See Me as I really am, that you may always have the joy of finding in Me all you could desire. The fulfillment of all you could desire in Master, Lord, or friend.

OCTOBER 5
NO CHANCE MEETINGS

"The LORD will watch over your coming and going both now and forevermore."
(PSALM 121:8 NIV 1984)

All of your activities, your comings and goings, are controlled by Me. Every visit is blessed by Me. Every walk is arranged by Me. A blessing on everything you do, on every conversation.

Every meeting is planned by Me. There are no chance meetings. All are blessed.

This is true not only now, in the hour of your difficulty, but is true now and forevermore.

Being led by the Spirit is proof that you are children of God. "For all who are led by the Spirit of God are children of God" (Romans 8:14 NLT). And "if we are children, then we are heirs — heirs of God" (Romans 8:17a NIV 1984).

What a heritage! Heirs — no possibility of being disinherited. "Heirs of God and co-heirs with Christ, if indeed we share in his sufferings in order that we may also share in his glory" (Romans 8:17 NIV 1984).

So your suffering has its purpose. It is proof that you are God's child. It leads to perfection of character (sharing in His glory), and to union with Me. And with God, too. Think about, and meditate on, the indescribable joy of this truth.

OCTOBER 6
A CHILD'S HAND

Dear Lord, we cling to You.

Yes, cling. Your faith shall be rewarded. Don't you know what it means to feel a little trusting hand in yours, to know a child's confidence in you?

Doesn't that bring out your love and desire to protect him, to care for him? Think about what My heart feels when in your helplessness, you turn to Me, clinging, desiring My love and protection.

No matter how many faults and weaknesses you have, would you fail that child? Could I fail you?

Just know that is not possible. Know that all is well. You must not doubt. You must be sure. There is no miracle I cannot perform, nothing that I cannot do. No eleventh-hour rescue I cannot accomplish.

OCTOBER 7
REJOICE AT WEAKNESS

*"Savior, breathe forgiveness o'er us.
All our weakness Thou dost know."*
("LEAD US, HEAVENLY FATHER, LEAD US,"
JAMES EDMUNDSTON, 1821)

Yes! I know everything! Every cry for mercy. Every sigh of weariness. Every plea for help. Every sorrow over failure. Every weakness.

I am with you through it all. My tender sympathy is yours. My strength is yours.

Rejoice at your weakness, My children. "My strength is made perfect in weakness" (2 Corinthians 12:9 NKJV). When you are weak, then I am strong. Strong to help, to cure, to protect.

Trust Me, My children. I know *everything*. I am beside you. Strong, strong, strong to save. Lean on My love, and know that all is well.

OCTOBER 8
THE DARK PLACES

"Jesus, the very thought of Thee
with Sweetness fills us."
("JESUS, THE VERY THOUGHT OF THEE,"
ADAPTED FROM SAINT BERNARD OF
CLAIRVAUX, EARLY 12TH CENTURY)

Yes. Love Me until just to think of Me means joy and rapture. Such happiness at the mere thought of One very near and dear.

The thought of Me is the salve for all sorrows. By thinking of Me and speaking to Me, you can always find healing for all physical, mental, and spiritual afflictions.

Are doubts and fears in your hearts? Then think about Me, speak to Me. Instead of those doubts and fears, such sweet joy beyond any joy on earth will flow into your hearts and beings.

This never fails. Never doubt it. Courage. Courage. Courage. Fear nothing. Rejoice even in the darkest places. Rejoice.

OCTOBER 9
LOVE ME MORE

"Jesus, our Lord ... We Thee adore!
Oh, make us love Thee more and more."
("JESUS, MY LORD, MY GOD, MY ALL,"
HENRY A. COLLINS, 1854)

Yes! I desire to draw you closer and closer to Me with cords of love: the love of the sinner for the Savior, of the rescued for the Rescuer, of the sheep for the loving Shepherd, of the child for her Father.

There are so many ties of love to bind you to Me.

Each experience in your life makes its own particular demand on Me, whether it is one of joy or sorrow, of difficulty or success, hardship or ease, or of danger or safety. Each serves to answer the prayer: "Make me love Thee more and more."

OCTOBER 10
EXTRA WORK

*Our Lord and our God. Help us
through poverty to plenty. Through
unrest to rest, through sorrow to joy,
through weakness to power.*

I am your helper. All these blessings await you at the end of your present path. So trust and know that I am leading you.

Step into each unknown day with a firm step of confidence in Me. Regard every obligation and every interruption as being assigned by Me.

You are My servant. Serve Me as simply, cheerfully, and willingly as you expect others to serve you.

Do you find fault with the employee who avoids extra work, who complains about being pulled off of one job to do another one he likes less? Do you feel as if you are poorly served by someone like that?

What about Me? Isn't that the way you frequently serve Me? Think about this. Take this to heart, and examine your day's work with this in mind.

OCTOBER 11
SHAME AND DISTRESS

"I will praise the LORD *at all times.*
I will constantly speak his praises.
I prayed to the LORD, *and he answered me.*
He freed me from all my fears.
Those who look to him for help will be
radiant with joy;
no shadow of shame will darken their faces."
(PSALM 34:1, 4–5 NLT)

You see, My children, that even in distress, the first step is praise. Before you cry out in distress, praise the Lord, even when troubles seem to overwhelm you.

This sequence is My divine order of approach. Always observe this. Even in your greatest distress, search until you find a reason to be thankful. Then praise Me and thank Me.

By doing this, you have established a line of communication between you and Me. Let your cry of distress follow along that line.

Then you will find that I will do My part, and you will certainly be delivered. Oh, how happy your heart will be! As the result of looking to Me, your spirit will be lightened and your burden will be rolled away.

The shame and distress will be lifted, too. That is always the second step. First, get in right standing with Me, and then you also will be put in right standing in the eyes of men.

OCTOBER 12
YOU ARE MY JOY

"They were Yours, You gave them to Me, and they have kept Your word."
(JOHN 17:6 NKJV)

Remember, just as you thank God for Me, I thank God for His gift of you to Me. In the hour of My agony on earth, one note of joy rose above the pain: the thought of those who were given to Me by My Father and who had kept My Word.

They had not yet done great deeds in and for My name, even though they would later. They were doers of My Word, not hearers only (James 1:22). In their daily lives and tasks, they just kept My Word.

You, too, can bring joy to My heart by faithful service. Faithful service in the little things. Be faithful.

Do your simple tasks for Me.

THE SCULPTOR'S SKILL

"Lord, [we] believe; help [our] unbelief!"
(Mark 9:24 NKJV). Lord, hear our prayers
and let our cries come to You.

As I have told you before, I will answer your prayers as you walk along the road of praise. Yes, indeed! I will help your unbelief. In answer to your prayers, I will grant you so great a faith, such an increasingly great faith, that each day you can look back from your greater perspective and see the faith you had the day before as almost unbelief.

The beauty of My kingdom is its growth. In that kingdom, there is always progress, going from strength to strength, "from glory to glory" (2 Corinthians 3:18 NKJV). Be in My kingdom and of My kingdom, and there can be no standing still. Eternal life, abundant life, is promised to everyone in it and of it.

Don't waste time over your failures and shortcomings. Consider the lessons learned from them as rungs in the ladder. Step up, and disregard any thought about how the rung was made. My children, so long as it served its purpose, does it really matter whether it was made from joy or sorrow, success or failure, or from health or hurt?

Learn another lesson. The sculptor who finds a defective slab of marble sets it aside. Because it has not been worked on, it may think of itself as being perfect. It may smugly, scornfully, look down on the marble the sculptor is cutting and shaping into perfection. My children, learn a lesson for your lives from this.

OCTOBER 14
THE SACRIFICE

"Here he is, God's Passover Lamb! He forgives the sins of the world!" (John 1:29 MSG)

Christ, our Passover, was sacrificed for us" (1 Corinthians 5:7 NKJV). I am the Lamb of God. Place upon Me your sins, your failures, and your shortcomings. My sacrifice has paid the debt for them all. I am the "one Mediator who can reconcile God and humanity — the man Christ Jesus" (1 Timothy 2:5 NLT).

Do not dwell upon the past. To do so makes My sacrifice meaningless.

No! You must realize that in Me you have everything: complete forgiveness, complete companionship, complete healing.

OCTOBER 15
ATTITUDE OF ABUNDANCE

Live in My secret place, and there the feeling is one of full satisfaction. Feel like there is an abundance. The storehouses of God are full to overflowing, but you must see this in your mind.

You must be sure of this before you can realize it in a material way.

Think thoughts of abundance. See yourselves as daughters of the King. I have told you this. Desire abundance for yourselves and for everyone you care about and want to help.

OCTOBER 16
THE IMPRISONED GOD

Our Lord, we praise You and
bless Your name forever.

Yes! Praise. The moment you praise, even during your most difficult times, your sorrow is turned to joy, your worry to praise, your outward circumstances are changed from disorder to order. From chaos to calm.

All reform must begin within you. No matter how limited your situation, or how modest your means, you can always look within yourselves. When you see something that is not in order there, work on making that right.

As all reform is from the inside out, you will always find that the outside has improved, too. To effect change by starting within you is to release the imprisoned God-power within you.

That power, once working, will immediately perform miracles. Then, indeed, your mourning shall be turned into joy.

OCTOBER 17
VISION BORN OF FAITH

Turn your eyes to gaze upon Me. Look away from squalid surroundings, from lack of beauty, and from the imperfections in yourselves and those around you. Then you who have the vision born of faith will see everything you could desire in Me, everything you do desire in Me.

In your turmoil, see My calm, My rest. In your impatience, see My unfailing patience. In your lack and limitation, see My perfection.

Looking at Me, you will grow to be more like Me until people say to you, too, that you have been with Jesus (Acts 4:13).

As you grow to be more like Me, you will be empowered to do the things I do, "and even greater works, because I am going to be with the Father" (John 14:12 NLT).

From that place of abiding with Me, free from humanity's limitations, I can clothe you with the all-conquering, all miracle-working power of your divine Brother and Ally.

OCTOBER 18
LONELINESS

"Then all his disciples
deserted him and ran away."
(MARK 14:50 NLT)

Down through the ages, all the simple acts of faithful devotion, of obeying when it's hard, and of loving service, help to make up for the loneliness I suffered when My disciples deserted Me.

I completely understood the Father's desire to save, His rejection by mankind, and that His reason and purpose would be misconstrued. So, how could I think that I should not experience that desertion as well?

My children, learn the lessons contained in these truths. First, learn that I know what loneliness, desertion, and solitude mean. Secondly, learn that every faithful act of yours is a comfort to My heart. Also learn that is was to those deserters that I gave the task of bringing My message to all mankind. To those deserters, those fearful men, I gave My power to heal, and to raise people from the dead (Matthew 10:8).

I do not use earthly successes for the great work of My kingdom. "All his disciples deserted him and ran away." Learn that I tenderly understand and forgive human weakness. Not until a man has failed has he learned true humility. And it is only the humble who can inherit the earth (Matthew 5:5 NLT).

OCTOBER 19
HEAR MY ANSWER

"Hear [our] prayer, O LORD;
let [our] cry for help come to you."
(PSALM 102:1 NIV 1984)

The cry of the human soul is never unheard. It is never that God does not hear the cry, but that man fails to hear the response.

The human cry and God's response are just like parts of a machine which are made to fit together and to work in perfect harmony.

But man treats this cry as if it were a separate thing, to be heard, or not, as it pleases God. Man does not realize that God's response was there throughout eternity just waiting for the cry. It is only man's failure to pay attention, or to listen, that keeps him unaware of the response, and neither saved nor helped by it.

OCTOBER 20
NO BURDEN ANNOYS

Our Lord and our God. "Let it be done to
[us] according to what you have said."
(LUKE 1:38B AMP)

Simple acceptance of My will is the key to divine revelation. It will result in both holiness and happiness. The way to the cross may be a way of sorrow, but at the foot of the cross, the burdens of sin and earthly desire are rolled away.

Accepting My Father's will in all things is the yoke you must take upon you (Matthew 11:29), but that yoke is fitted to each servant's shoulders individually. From the moment you take that yoke upon you, no burden annoys you or weighs you down.

Accept and welcome My will in everything, not only in the big decisions of life. Try to see that I also use each interruption and each task, no matter how small, to fulfill My divine intent.

Accept My will, and say "Thank You" for it. Do this until it becomes a habit, and the resulting joy will transform and transfigure your lives.

OCTOBER 21
A LOVE FEAST

"Behold, I stand at the door and knock. If anyone hears My voice and opens the door, I will come in to him and dine with him, and he with Me."
(REVELATION 3:20 NKJV)

See, My children, My knocking upon the door does not depend upon your worthiness, although it is in response to your heart's longing for Me.

Listen and keep on listening. "If anyone hears My voice." Again, this does not depend upon your worthiness. All that is needed is the ear inclined to catch My voice, and to hear the sound of My gentle knocking.

Then listen: "If anyone hears My voice and opens the door, I will come in to him and dine with him, and he with Me."

What a feast! You think it would have been pure joy to have been present at the marriage feast of Cana of Galilee (John 2:1–11). Or to have been one of My disciples in the Upper Room seated with Me at the Last Supper (Matthew 26:20–29). Or one of the two believers with whom I shared a meal in Emmaus (Luke 24:13–35). Or one of the few for whom I prepared that lakeside feast (John 21:1–14 NIV 1984).

At each of these feasts, although they were provided by God and He shared them with His companions, you could not have known the rapture that you can know as you hear My knocking and My voice, and then open the door, and welcome Me into My feast.

A feast of the most tender companionship, of divine sustenance. Truly a Love Feast!

OCTOBER 22
HOME-BUILDING

You are building up an unshakable faith. Furnish the quiet places of your souls now.

Fill them with all that is harmonious and good, beautiful and lasting.

Home-build in the Spirit now, and your waiting time will be well spent.

OCTOBER 23
HILL OF SACRIFICE

You must trust to the end. You must be ready to go on trusting until the final hour.

You must *know* even when you cannot *see* (Hebrews 11:1). Like My servant Abraham, you must be ready to climb the very hill of sacrifice, to go to the very last moment before you see My deliverance (Genesis 22:1–13).

This final test has to come to all who walk by faith. You must rely on Me alone.

Look to no other arm to save you (Isaiah 59:1), look for no other help. Trust in the spiritual forces of the unseen, not in those you see. Trust and do not fear.

OCTOBER 24
SALT OF THE EARTH

Our Lord, we bless You and thank You
for Your keeping power.

Yes! "Kept by the power of God" (1 Peter 1:5 NKJV) is a promise and assurance that holds joy and beauty for the believing soul.

This "keeping," which means safety and security, is wonderful. There is also the "keeping" which implies life, freshness, purity—the being kept "unstained by the world" (James 1:27 HCSB).

Then there is the "keeping" that I promise to those I call the "salt of the earth" (Matthew 5:13).

"You are the salt of the earth. But if the salt loses its saltiness, how can it be made salty again? It is no longer good for anything, except to be thrown out and trampled underfoot" (Matthew 5:13 NIV 2011).

That keeping power is only realized by those in close contact with Me. It is that keeping power which maintains the salt at its freshest and best, and also preserves from corruption that portion of the world in which I place it.

What an achievement! In this case, work is accomplished not by salt doing anything, but simply by its being, by its very essence.

OCTOBER 25
NO UNEMPLOYMENT

The way to be victorious over the material, the earthly, which all of My disciples ought to know, is learned by conquering the desires of the flesh and the "self" in each of you.

Therefore, seek to conquer in all things. Regard this as extremely clear guidance. Circumstances are adverse. Both worldly power and money need to be coming to you.

Therefore, each day you must seek to conquer your "self" more and more. Although you may not see it, you will certainly be gaining victory over worldly forces and powers.

If man realized this, there would be no unemployment.

If someone does not have a job, let him make himself a conquering force. Let him begin by defeating all evil within himself, then in his home, then in all around him. He will become a force that will be needed and must be employed.

There are no idle hours in My kingdom. Waiting may seem to be a time of inactivity as far as the outer world is concerned. But it can be, and should be, a time of great activity in the inner life and the immediate surroundings of the believer.

OCTOBER 26
DESERTERS

You must believe completely and totally. My love cannot stand anything less. I am so often "wounded in the house of my friends" (Zechariah 13:6 NKJV). Do you think the spitting and contempt of My enemies, the insults and abuse, hurt Me? No!

"Then everyone deserted him and fled" (Mark 14:50 NIV 1984). "I don't even know the man" (Matthew 26:72 NLT). These left their scars.

This is still true. It is not the unbelief of My enemies that hurts, but that My friends, who know Me and love Me, cannot go the distance with Me, and doubt My power to do everything I have said.

OCTOBER 27
DAYS OF VICTORY

I see how you are loving and how you are striving. I do not see your faults. I see how you overcome your particular battles, and I count it as a victory, a glad victory.

I do not compare it to the strenuous battles of My great saints.

For you it is a victory, and the angels rejoice, and your loved ones rejoice as much as heaven rejoices over any victory it sees.

My children, count the days of victory as very blessed days.

OCTOBER 28
DELIGHTFUL SURPRISES

Our Lord, we know that all is well. We trust
You for everything. We love You more and
more. We bow to Your will.

Do not bow like someone who is resigned to receiving some heavy blow which is about to fall, or to receiving some inevitable bad news.

Bow like a child bows, in anticipation of a delightful surprise being prepared for him by someone who loves him.

Bow this way, just waiting to hear Me lovingly tell you to look up, and see the glory and joy and wonder of your surprise.

OCTOBER 29
YOUR SUCCESS

Never measure success by how much money you have. That is not the standard of My kingdom. Your success is measured by how much of My will and mind you have revealed to those around you.

Your success is how much of My will that those around you have seen worked out in your lives.

OCTOBER 30
THE HARDEST LESSON

Wait, and you shall realize the joy of one who can be calm and wait, knowing that all is well. The last and hardest lesson is that of waiting. So wait.

I almost said tonight, "Forgive Me, children, that I allow this extra burden to rest upon you even for so short a time."

I want you to know that from the moment you placed everything in My hands, and looked to no one else for help, from that moment I have taken the quickest way possible to work out your salvation, and to free you.

You have had to be taught so much in order to avoid future disaster. But the Friend with whom you stand by the grave of failure, of dead ambitions, of surrendered desires, that Friend is a Friend for all time.

Use this waiting time to cement the friendship with Me and to increase your knowledge of Me.

OCTOBER 31
THE VOICE AGAIN

"Thy word is a lamp unto my feet, and a light unto my path."
(PSALM 119:105 KJV)

Yes! My Word, the Scriptures. Read them. Study them. Store them in your hearts. Use them as you would use a lamp to guide your footsteps.

But remember, My children, My Word is even more than that. It is the voice that speaks to your hearts, that inner consciousness that reveals Me.

It is the voice that speaks to you intimately, personally, in this sacred evening time. It is even more than that. It is I, your Lord and Friend.

"So the Word became human and made his home among us" (John 1:14 NLT). Truly, a lamp to your feet and a light to your path.

NOVEMBER 1
PRAYER OF JOY

Joy is the messenger, dear Lord, that
carries our prayers to You.

Prayer can be like incense, rising ever higher and higher, or it can be like fog clinging to the ground, never once soaring.

The eye that sees everything, the ear that hears everything, knows *every* cry.

But the prayer of real faith is the prayer of joy, that sees and knows the heart of love it rises to greet, and that is so certain that it will receive a glad response.

NOVEMBER 2
SPEND

Give, give, give. Always keep an empty vessel for Me to fill.

In the future, use everything for Me, and give away everything you cannot use.

Those who die leaving wealth behind die very poor indeed! Wealth is to use, to spend, for Me.

Use it as you go. Delight to use it.

NOVEMBER 3
NO LIMIT

Unlimited supply, that is My law. How sad! The supply is unlimited but the poor channels are blocked. Please feel and know to the depth of your being that there is no limit to My power.

But people ask for such inferior and trivial things, and in doing so, commit blasphemy. Don't you see how you hurt Me? I desire to give you a gift, and if you are content with the inferior and the trivial and the vile, then you are insulting Me, the giver.

"If you remain in me and my words remain in you, you may ask for anything you want, and it will be granted!" (John 15:7b NLT). It is My work, not yours, to consider how I can fulfill this promise … Have a big faith, and expect big things, and you will get big things.

NOVEMBER 4
I AM BESIDE YOU

"In Your presence is fullness of joy; at Your
right hand are pleasures forevermore."
(PSALM 16:11 NKJV)

Do not seek to experience this fullness of joy as
the result of effort. You cannot force this to
happen. That's like thinking that the joy you feel in
a friend's presence results from forcing yourself to
feel that way.

Call out My name often. "Jesus."

Calling out My name does not really cause Me
to appear. I am always beside you. But it removes
the scales from your eyes (Acts 9:18), and you see
Me.

It is like a squeeze of a loved one's hand that
brings an answering squeeze. Then a thrill of joy
follows, a real, and a joyful sense of being so close.

NOVEMBER 5
SECOND ADVENT

Jesus, comforter of everyone who is sorrowful, help us to bring Your comfort into the hearts and lives of every person whom You long to comfort through us. Use us, Lord. The years may be many or few. Put us where we can best serve You, and influence the most people for You.

The world would be brought to Me so soon, so soon, if only everyone who acknowledges Me as Lord, as Christ, gave themselves unconditionally to be used by Me.

I could use *each* human body as mightily as I used My own body as a channel for divine love and power.

I do not delay My second coming. My *followers* delay it.

If each person lived for Me, by Me, in Me, allowing Me to live in him, to use him to express the divine through him as I expressed it while on earth, then the world would have been drawn to Me long ago, and I would have come to claim My own.

Therefore, My children, seek to live knowing no other desire than to express Me, and to show My love to your world.

NOVEMBER 6
GOD IN ACTION

Power is not as overwhelming a force as it sounds, something you call to help you, to intervene in times of crisis. No! *Power is just God in action.*

Therefore, whenever a servant of Mine, no matter how weak he may be physically, allows God to work through him, then everything he does is *powerful.*

Keep this thought in mind on the days you seem to accomplish little. Try to see that it is not you, but the divine Spirit in you. As I have told you before, all you have to do is to crucify "self." A very powerful axe in the hand of a master accomplishes a lot. The same tool in the hand of a weak child accomplishes nothing. So see, it is not the instrument that matters, but the Master Hand that wields it.

Remember, no day is wasted in which some spiritual truth becomes more clear. No day is lost which you have given to Me to use. My use of it may not have been apparent to you. Leave that to Me. "Those who remain in me, and I in them, will produce much fruit" (John 15:5b NLT). The fruit is not produced by the branches, although the branches may bear it proudly. It is the work of the vine that sends its life-giving sap through those branches. "Yes, I am the vine; you are the branches" (John 15:5a NLT).

NOVEMBER 7
"SELF" KILLS POWER

If you live with Me, desiring only My will and to do My work, then My Spirit cannot help but to pass through the channel of your life into the lives of others.

Many people think of it as humility to say that they do little and are of little value to My world. To think *that* is pride.

What if the water pipe were to say: "I do so little, I wish I could be of more use"? The reply would be: "It is not you, but the water that passes through you, that saves and blesses. All you have to do is make sure there is nothing blocking the way that prevents the water from flowing through."

The only blockage there can be in *your* channel is "self." Keep that out, and know that My Spirit is flowing through. Therefore, everyone will be better off for having come into contact with both of you, because you are channels. Once you understand this, you will think it is natural to know they are being helped, not by you, but by My Spirit flowing through you as a channel.

NOVEMBER 8
WIPE THE SLATE

*"But one thing I do: Forgetting what is
behind and straining toward what is ahead,
I press on toward the goal ..."*
(PHILIPPIANS 3:13B–14A NIV 1984)

Forget the past. Only remember its happy days. Wipe the slate of your memories with love, which will erase everything in which love clearly had no part. You must forget your failures — your failures and those of others. Wipe them out of your memory book.

I did not die upon the cross for man to bear the burdens of his sins himself. "He personally carried our sins in his body on the cross" (1 Peter 2:24a NLT).

If you do not forget the sins of others, and I carry them, then you add to My sorrows.

NOVEMBER 9
WONDERFUL FRIENDSHIP

Think of Me as a friend, but also realize the wonder of the friendship. Man gives Me worship and honor, obedience and loyalty. But, as soon as he also gives Me loving understanding, then he becomes My friend, just as I am his friend.

It is not merely a question of what I can do for you, although that is part of it. But it is also about what we can do for each other. What you can do for Me.

Your service becomes so different when you feel I count on your great friendship to do this or that for Me.

Spend more time, a lot more time, thinking about this idea of you as My friends, and of the sweetness of My knowing where I can turn for love, for understanding, and for help.

NEW FORCES

Remember that life's difficulties and troubles are not intended to hinder your progress, but to increase your speed. You must call new forces, new powers into action.

Whatever it is must be surmounted, overcome. Remember this.

It is like a race. Nothing must intimidate you. Do not let a difficulty conquer you. You must conquer it.

My strength will be there waiting for you. Put all of your thoughts and all of your power into action. Nothing is too small to be faced and overcome. To push *small* difficulties aside is to ask for big troubles.

Rise to conquer. It is the path to victory I want you to follow. There can be no failure with Me.

"Now to Him who is able to keep you from stumbling, and to present you faultless before the presence of His glory with exceeding joy ..." (Jude 1:24 NKJV).

NOVEMBER 11
HEAVEN'S COLORS

Looking back, you will see that every step was planned. Leave everything to Me. Each stone in the mosaic fits into the perfect pattern, which has been designed by the Master Artist.

It is all so wonderful!

But the colors are from heaven's palette, so that your eyes cannot stand to look at the finished work until you are in paradise with Me.

So, stone by stone, you see, and trust the pattern to the designer.

NOVEMBER 12
THE VOICELESS CRY

Jesus, hear us. "*And let our cry come unto Thee*" (*1928* Book of Common Prayer).

The voiceless cry that comes from broken hearts is heard above all of the music of heaven.

It is not the arguments of theologians that solve the problems of a questioning heart, but the cry of that heart to Me, and the certainty I have heard it.

NOVEMBER 13
EVERY PROBLEM SOLVED

Man has such strange ideas regarding the meaning of My invitation, "Come to Me" (Matthew 11:28). It has been interpreted too often as a command to pay a tribute owed to a Creator or a debt owed to a Savior.

"Come to Me" contains in it a wealth of meaning which far surpasses even that. "Come to Me" for the solution to every problem, for the calming of every fear, for everything you need — physical, mental, and spiritual.

Sick? Come to Me for health. Homeless? Ask Me for a home. Friendless? Claim a friend. Hopeless? A refuge.

"Come to Me" for everything.

NOVEMBER 14
DISHONEST WAYS

Life is not easy, My children. Man has made of life something besides what My Father meant it to be.

Ways that were meant to be straight paths have been made by man into ways that are dishonest and evil, filled with obstacles and stones of difficulty.

NOVEMBER 15
BY MY SPIRIT

People may think that I worked miracles only in the past. That is not so. Wherever someone trusts in Me completely, and allows Me to choose the exact moment, then My miracle-working power is revealed. It is as marvelously revealed today as it ever was when I was on earth. That power is as clear today as it was when My apostles were set free (Acts 12:1–19; 16:16–40) or when I worked miracles of wonder and healing through them (Matthew 10:8).

Trust in Me. Have infinite faith in Me, and you will see this is true. And seeing this, you will give Me all the glory. Remember, and say to yourselves often: "It is not by force nor by strength, but by my Spirit, says the Lord of Heaven's Armies" (Zechariah 4:6b NLT).

Seriously think about all I accomplished on earth, and then say to yourselves, "He, our Lord and our Friend, can do this in our lives now."

Apply these miracles to your present-day needs, and know that your help and salvation are certain.

NOVEMBER 16
UNION IS POWER

"For where two or three come together in my name, there am I with them."
(MATTHEW 18:20 NIV 1984)

Always claim that promise. Know that it is true that whenever two people who love Me come together, I am the third. Never limit that promise.

When you two are together in My name, united by one bond in My Spirit, I am there. This is always true, not just when you get together to call on Me and hear My voice.

Just think how powerful that union can be because of My presence. Once again, it is the lesson of the power that follows *two united to serve Me*.

NOVEMBER 17
QUIET LIVES

"Well done, good and faithful servant ...
Enter into the joy of your lord."
(MATTHEW 25:21 NKJV)

These words are whispered in the ears of many people the world passes by and does not recognize. So often, these words are not said to the great or the famous, but to the quiet followers who serve Me inconspicuously, yet faithfully, who bear their cross bravely while putting on a happy face. Thank Me for quiet lives.

In part, these words speak of passing into a fuller spiritual life. Duty faithfully done for Me means entering into a life of joy — My joy, the joy of your Lord. The world may never see the humble, patient, quiet service, but I see it. My reward is not earth's fame, earth's wealth, or earth's pleasures, but divine joy.

This is My reward, whether here or there, in the earthly realm or spiritual realm. The joy that carries an exquisite thrill in the midst of pain and poverty and suffering. The joy which I said no man could take from you (John 16:22). Earth has no pleasure, no reward, that can give man that joy. It is known only to those who love Me and are My friends.

This joy may come not only as a reward for serving Me. It may also be the reward for suffering bravely and patiently.

Suffering endured with Me must ultimately bring joy, as does all real contact with Me. So live with Me in that kingdom of joy, My kingdom, whether the gateway is through service or suffering.

NOVEMBER 18
DAZZLING GLORY

"Arise, shine; for your light has come! And the glory of the Lord is risen upon you."
(ISAIAH 60:1 NKJV)

The glory of the Lord is the beauty of His character. It is risen upon you when you understand it, although on earth you can only do so in part (1 Corinthians 13:9–12).

The beauty of the purity and love of God is too dazzling for people to see fully.

The glory of the Lord is also risen upon you when you reflect that glory in your lives. When in love, patience, service, purity, whatever it may be, you reveal to the world some characteristic of the Father, an assurance that you have been with Me, your Lord and Savior (Acts 4:13).

NOVEMBER 19
HILLS OF THE LORD

"I lift up my eyes to the hills — where does my help come from? My help comes from the LORD, *the Maker of heaven and earth."*
(PSALM 121:1–2, A SONG OF ASCENTS, NIV 1984)

Yes! Always raise your eyes — from earth's depravity, selfishness, and lies — to the hills of the Lord. From poverty, lift your eyes to the help of the Lord.

In moments of weakness, lift your eyes to the hills of the Lord.

Train your vision by constantly having this long view. Train it to see more and more, further and further, until distant mountain peaks seem familiar.

The hills of the Lord. The hills where your help comes from. A parched earth looks to the hills for its rivers, its streams, its life. In the same way, you must look to the hills. From those hills comes help. Help from the Lord — who made heaven and earth.

So, for all of your spiritual needs, look to the Lord who made heaven. And for all your material needs, look to Me, the owner of all of this, the Lord who made the earth.

NOVEMBER 20
MYSTERIES

Your hope is in the Lord (Psalm 39:7b). Set your hopes on Me. Know that whatever the future may hold, it will hold more and more of Me. Therefore, what else can your future be but happy and full of joy? So in heaven, or on earth, wherever you may be, your path must truly be one of delight.

Do not try to find answers to the mysteries of the world. Learn to know Me more and more, and in that knowledge, you will have all the answers you need here. And when you see Me face-to-face, in that purely spiritual world, you will have no need to ask. In heaven, as on earth, all of your answers will be in Me.

Remember, I was the answer in time to all of man's questions about My Father and His laws. More than knowing theology, know Me. I am the Word of God (John 1:1, 14 NIV 1984). All you need to know about God, you know in Me. If someone does not know Me, all of your explanations will fall on an unresponsive heart.

NOVEMBER 21
RADIATE JOY

You must not only rejoice, but your joy must be evident. Known by everyone. A candle must not be put under a basket, but set on a candlestick so that it may give light to everyone in the house (Matthew 5:15).

People must see and know your joy, and seeing it, know beyond the shadow of a doubt that it arises from trusting in Me, from living with Me.

My way is not the difficult, tedious way of calmly accepting a situation that is bad but cannot be changed. When I entered Jerusalem, I knew full well that scorn and abuse and death awaited Me. Yet I entered to shouts of "Hosanna!" and with a triumphal procession (Mark 11:1–10 NIV 1984). It was not just a few "lost cause" followers sneaking into the city with Me. There was not a hint of sadness in what I said to My disciples at the Last Supper (Mark 14:17–25), and when we "had sung a hymn, [we] went out to the Mount of Olives" (Mark 14:26 NIV 1984).

So trust. So conquer. So rejoice. Love puts everything in a different light. Love takes the sting out of the winds of adversity.

Love. Love. Love for Me. The awareness of My presence and the presence of My Father. We are One (John 10:30), and He — God — is love (1 John 4:8).

NOVEMBER 22
ONLY LOVE LASTS

"If I speak in the tongues of men and of angels, but have not love, I am only a resounding gong or a clanging cymbal."
(1 CORINTHIANS 13:1 NIV 1984)

Realize that only love matters. Only what is done in love lasts, for God is love, and only the work of God remains.

Consider the fame of the world, the applause given to the one who speaks with the tongues of men and of angels, and who attracts admiration and compels attention. All of these are prone to what is fleeting and truly worthless if they lack that God-quality, love.

Think about how a smile or word of love goes winging on its way, with God-power, however simple it may seem. In contrast, the mighty words of an eloquent speaker can fall fruitless to the ground. The true test of all work and words is: "Are they inspired by love?"

If people only saw how meaningless so much of their activity is! So much work which is done in My name is not acknowledged by Me. With respect to love, banish everything that is not loving from your hearts and lives. In this way, you shall bear much fruit (John 15:8), and "your love for one another will prove to the world that you are my disciples" (John 13:35 NLT).

NOVEMBER 23
EARTH'S RAGES

"Here on earth you will have many trials
and sorrows. But take heart, because I
have overcome the world."
(JOHN 16:33 NLT)

Then, My children, you may ask why you must have trials and sorrows if I have overcome the world.

As you know, My overcoming was never for Myself, but was for you, for My children. I overcame each temptation, each difficulty as it presented itself.

The powers of evil were stretched to their limit to find a way to break Me. They failed. But how they failed was known only to Me, and to My Father, who could read My undiscouraged spirit. The world, and even My own followers, would see a lost cause. Seeing Me being verbally abused, spit on, and scourged, they would consider Me defeated. How could they know My spirit was free, unbroken, unharmed?

And so, as I had come to show God to man, I must show him God unconquered, unharmed, and untouched by evil and its power. Man could not see My spirit untouched, having risen above earthly rages and hatreds, into the secret place of the Father (Psalm 91:1 NIV 1984). But *man* could see My risen body and learn from that, that even the final attempt by man had been powerless to touch Me.

Take heart in that, because you must share My trials and sorrows. For evil to leave you unchallenged, it must mean that you are evil. If evil challenges you, if trials bear down heavily upon you, it is because you are on My side. As My friends, you are exposed to evil's hatred.

But be of good cheer (John 16:33). You walk with Me. I conquered evil at every turn, although man could only see it proven beyond any doubt when I rose from the dead. And in *My* conquering power, you walk unharmed today.

NOVEMBER 24
SACRIFICE TO SAVE

Accept each day's events as work you can do for Me. When taken with that spirit, a blessing will be present in all you do. Offering your daily service to Me in this way, you are sharing in My life-work, and therefore helping Me to save My world.

You may not see it, but the power of sacrifice made on behalf of another is redemptive beyond man's ability to understand here on earth.

NOVEMBER 25
THE HEAVENLY BEGGAR

"Behold, I stand at the door and knock."
(REVELATION 3:20A NKJV)

Oh, deeply and thoroughly consider these words again, and discover My great humility from them.

There is also a gracious invitation for those who long to find a happiness, a rest, a satisfaction they have never found in the world and its pursuits. To them, the answer to their search is My pleading, "Come to me … and I will give you rest" (Matthew 11:28 NIV 1984).

There are those who feel no need for Me, who stubbornly reject Me, who shut the doors of their hearts so that I may not enter. But I go to them in tender, humble longing. Even when I find everything all closed up and barricaded, I stand there a beggar, knocking, knocking. The Heavenly Beggar in His great humility.

For those who have shut you out or forgotten you, don't think that now they must wait, that you don't need them. No! Remember the Heavenly Beggar and learn about humility from Me.

Also learn the value of each person's happiness and peace and rest to Me, his God. And learn, and as you learn, pray to imitate the divine unrest until a soul finds rest and peace in Me.

NOVEMBER 26
MY BEAUTY

The prophet Isaiah understood the truth of what I said centuries later: "He who has ears to hear, let him hear!" (Matthew 11:15 NKJV), which could as easily be expressed as "He who has eyes to see, let him see."

The God who was to be born on earth was not to be housed in a body so beautiful that men would follow and adore Him for the beauty of His face.

No! He would be one whom the world would despise. But to the seeing eye, the Spirit dwelling in that body would be so beautiful that it lacked nothing. "He had no beauty or majesty to attract us to him, nothing in his appearance that we should desire him" (Isaiah 53:2b NIV 1984).

Pray that you will have a seeing eye to see the beauty of My character, of My Spirit. No, even more than that, as men by faith saw the beauty of the Trinity in the One who had "no beauty or majesty," so you should pray to have that faith to see the beauty of My love in My dealings with you, in My actions. Pray until you, with the eyes of faith, will see all you could desire in what the world will distort into cruelty and harshness.

Know Me. Talk to Me. Let Me talk to you so that I may make clear to your loving hearts what now seems mysterious and without purpose (having "no beauty or majesty").

NOVEMBER 27
NOT FRUSTRATED

Not our wills but Yours, O Lord
(adapted from Luke 22:42).

Man has so often misunderstood what I meant by this. I do not want anyone to lay their will on My altar grudgingly. I want you to desire and love My will, because that is where both your happiness and rest for your spirit lie.

Whenever you feel that you cannot leave the choice to Me, then pray, not to be able to accept My will, but to know Me more and love Me more. With knowing and loving Me more will come the certainty that I know best, and that I want only the best for you and yours.

Anyone who thinks that I wish to frustrate their plans shows how little they know Me. So often, I am answering their own prayers in the best and quickest way.

THE WAY OF THE SPIRIT

Jesus, we come to You with joy.

The joy of meeting with Me should fill your lives more and more. And it will. First of all, both your lives must be narrowed down more and more, into an inner-circle life with Me. And then, as that friendship becomes more and more consuming, more and more intertwined, then the circle of your interests will gradually widen.

For now, do not think of it as a narrow life. I have My purpose, My loving purpose, in separating you from other work and other interests for the time being.

To get to the inner-circle life with Me, you should not start with large interests and a desire for great activities and world movements. That is really the wrong way. That is why so often, when a soul does find Me through these activities and interests, I have to begin our friendship by cutting away the ties that bind it to the outer, wider circle. When it has gained strength and learned its lesson in the inner circle, it can then widen its life, this time working from the inside out, and then taking the inner-circle influence to each contact, to each friendship.

And this is to be your way of life.

This is the way of the Spirit. Man so often misunderstands this.

NOVEMBER 29
WHEN TWO AGREE

"... if two of you agree."
(MATTHEW 18:19 NKJV)

I am the Truth (John 14:6). Every word of Mine is true (2 Samuel 22:31). Every promise of Mine shall be fulfilled.

First, gather "together in My name" (Matthew 18:20 NKJV). Be bound by a common loyalty to Me, and desire only to do My will.

Then, when all of this is true, I am also present, a self-invited guest. And when I am there and one with you, joining My voice with yours in prayer and petition, making your demands My demands, then it follows that the request is granted.

But perhaps what man has failed to realize is *everything* that lies behind these words. For two to agree about the wisdom of a request, to be certain it *should* be granted, and *will* be granted (if it should be), is not the same as two agreeing to pray that request.

NOVEMBER 30
FROM SELF TO GOD

"The eternal God is your refuge ..."
(DEUTERONOMY 33:27A NIV 1984)

A place to flee to, a sanctuary. An escape from misunderstanding, *from yourself.* You can get away from others into the quiet of your own being, but from yourself, from the sense of your failure, your weakness, your sins and shortcomings, where can you go?

To the eternal God, your refuge. Until in His immensity you forget your smallness, your stinginess, your limitations.

Until your relief at being safe merges into the joy of appreciating your refuge, and you absorb the divine, and by absorbing, gain strength to conquer.

I am beside you. A very human Jesus who understands all of your weaknesses, and also sees your struggles and victories.

Remember, I was the companion of the weak. Ready to feed the hungry. Teaching My followers their responsibility toward everyone, not only those near and dear to them, but to the multitude.

Lord, "send the people away so they can go to the surrounding countryside and villages and buy themselves something to eat" (Mark 6:36 NIV 1984), said My disciples, with no sympathy for the fainting and exhausted men, women, and children.

But I taught that divine sympathy includes responsibility. "You give them something to eat" was My reply (Mark 6:37a NIV 1984). I taught that pity without a solution for the harm, or the need, is worthless.

"You give them something to eat." Wherever your sympathy goes, if possible, you must go there, too. Remember that when you are considering your own needs. Adopt this attitude for Me now so that it guides you as you weigh the needs of others against your own.

"A servant is not greater than his master" (John 13:16a NKJV), certainly not in spiritual accomplishments, and what I taught My disciples, *I* do.

So if you are fainting and needy by the lakeside of life, know that I will supply your needs, not grudgingly, but in full measure (Luke 6:38).

DECEMBER 2
THE IDEAL MAN

Take off your shoes and come close in silent awe and adoration. Come close, just as Moses drew near to the burning bush.

I give you the loving intimacy of being your friend, but I am also God. The wonder of our relationship, the miracle of your intimacy with Me, will mean so much more to you if you sometimes see the majestic figure of the Son of God.

Come close in absolute confidence. That is the most eloquent prayer. Come close. No crying out from far away even though I am a God clothed with majesty of fire. Come close. Come close, not as a beggar, but as a listener. I am the beggar, as I make My wishes known to you. For this majestic

God is your brother, too, longing so intensely that you would serve your fellow man, and longing, even more intensely, that you would be true to that vision that He has of you.

You speak about your fellow man as disappointing you, as falling short of the ideal you had of him. How do you think I feel? For every man, there is the ideal man I see in him. The man he could be, the man I would like him to be.

Consider how heartbroken I am when he fails to fulfill that promise. The disappointments of man may be great and many, but they are nothing compared to My disappointments. Remember this, and strive to be the friend I see in My vision of you.

DECEMBER 3
A JOURNEY WITH ME

Don't trouble your souls with puzzles you cannot solve. The solutions may never be shown to you until you have left this earthly life.

Remember what I have told you so often: "I have a lot more to tell you, but that would be too much for you now" (John 16:12 GWT). You can only proceed in your journey upward step by step, phase by phase.

The one thing you must be sure of is that it is a journey with Me. There does come a joy known to those who suffer with Me. But that joy is not the result of the suffering. Rather, it is the result of the close intimacy with Me to which the suffering drove you.

DECEMBER 4
MAN OF SORROWS

"He is despised and rejected by men, a Man of sorrows and acquainted with grief. And we hid, as it were, our faces from Him; He was despised, and we did not esteem Him."
(ISAIAH 53:3 NKJV)

The fact that these words strike a note of beauty in the hearts of those attuned to hear the beautiful truly shows that the heart recognizes the need for the Man of *Sorrows*. That it sees nothing detestable in One despised by the world. That it recognizes the vast difference between the values of heaven, and those of the world. Fame and approval are bestowed upon those the world considers great, while contempt and rejection are bestowed on the Son of God.

One of the things My disciples must always try to do is reject the values of the world, and judge only according to the values of heaven. Do not seek the praise and notice of men. These are not for you. You follow a despised Christ. See, the mob is booing, throwing stones, taunting; yet in that quiet "little flock" (Luke 12:32 KJV), there is a happiness and joy the abusive crowds could never know.

The mob follows behind the little flock, throwing stones and hurling insults. To outward appearances, that little flock, the small band of disciples, appears to be made up of men as mean, absurd, and worthy of contempt as the mob in pursuit. Be one of that flock, and there you feel the majesty of God in the presence of Him who was despised and rejected by men. But don't try to crown Him with wreaths upon His brow. Don't shout and applaud. These would only diminish His majesty.

In your darkest days, when human help fails, keep very close to the Man of Sorrows. Feel My hand of love squeeze yours in silent but complete understanding. I, too, was acquainted with grief. No heart can ache without My heart aching, too. "He was despised, and we did not esteem Him."

DECEMBER 5
LAW OF SUPPLY

The first law of giving is a spiritual law. Give to everyone you meet, or whose lives touch yours. Give of your prayers, your time, yourselves, your love, and your kind thoughts and words. You must practice *this* giving first.

Then, give of this world's goods and money, as they are given to you. It is wrong to give money and material things without first making it a habit (daily, hourly, increasingly more and more) of giving on the higher plane.

Give, give, give all of your best to everyone who needs it.

Be great givers — great givers. Give in the same way I said My Father in heaven gives. "He makes His sun rise on the evil and on the good, and sends rain on the just and on the unjust" (Matthew 5:45b NKJV). Remember, as I have told you before, give according to need, never according to what someone deserves. In giving with the aim of supplying a real need, you most closely resemble that Father in heaven, the Great Giver.

As you receive, you must supply the needs of those I bring to you. Not questioning, not limiting. Their closeness to you, their relationship with you, must never matter. Be guided solely by their need. Pray to become great givers.

DECEMBER 6
EXPECT TEMPTATION

Lord, give us power to conquer temptation as You conquered temptation in the wilderness (see Matthew 4:1–11).

The very first step towards conquering temptation is to *see* it as a temptation and divorce yourself from it.

Do not think of it as something that was caused by your weariness, or illness, or poverty, or anxiety, which might make you feel like you can justly excuse yourself for giving in. But first you must very clearly understand that when you have heard My voice (as though "the heavens were opened" [Matthew 3:16–17 NKJV]) and you are going to fulfill your calling to work for Me and to draw souls to Me, you must expect a ferocious attack from the evil one. He will try with all his might to frustrate you and to prevent your good work. Expect that.

Then, when these temptations come, small or large, you will recognize them as planned by evil to hinder Me. Then, out of your very love of Me, you will conquer.

DECEMBER 7
FOOD OF LIFE

*"I have food to eat that
you know nothing about."*
(JOHN 4:32 NIV 1984)

Those were My words to My disciples in the early days of My ministry. Later, I led them to a fuller understanding of that majestic union of a soul with God through which strength, life, and food pass from One to the other.

You eat meat to sustain the physical body. To do the will of God is the very strength and support of the spiritual life. Feed on *that* food.

A soul starves by failing to do My will, and failing to *delight* in doing My will. The world is always talking about bodies that are undernourished! What about the *souls* that are undernourished?

Make doing My will your meat, the source of your nourishment. Indeed, strength and power will come to you from that.

DECEMBER 8
MY KINGDOM

"... and greater works than these [you]
will do, because I go to My Father."
(JOHN 14:12 NKJV)

M ost of the people with whom I came into contact while I was on earth thought that My cause was a lost cause. Even My disciples did not wholly believe, and remained half-doubting, half-wondering. When they all deserted Me and ran away (Mark 14:50), it was not mainly due to their fear of My enemies. Rather, it was because they were certain that My mission, however beautiful they thought it was, had now failed.

In spite of everything I had taught them and, in spite of the revelation of the Last Supper, they had secretly felt certain that when the final moment came, and the hatred of the Pharisees was pronounced against Me, I would shout out a call to action, and that I would lead My many followers and establish My earthly kingdom. Even the disciples who had eyes to see My spiritual kingdom thought earthly forces had proven to be too strong for Me.

But with My resurrection came hope. Faith revived. They would remind each other of everything I had said. They would have the assurance of My divinity, of the fact that I am the Messiah. (They previously lacked that assurance and, without it, My work on earth was more difficult.) And they would have all My power in the unseen — the Holy Spirit — to help them.

Remember, I came to establish a kingdom — *the* Kingdom. Those who live in that kingdom are to do the work — greater works than I was able to do. Not a greater power shown, not a greater life lived, but that opportunities for works in My name would increase as men recognized My divinity. My work on earth was to gather around Me the core group of My kingdom, and to teach them the truths of My kingdom. Then they were to work and live in those truths.

YOUR SEARCH REWARDED

"Lord, everyone is looking for you!"
(MARK 1:37)

All men are looking for Me, but not all men know what they want. They are searching because they are dissatisfied, but they do not realize that they are searching for Me.

For those who seek, you can prove that you knew their search would end when they saw Me as they see how you live your life and endure trials, how you speak and how you love. If you are the means by which they realize this, count it as your greatest joy.

Learn from My example. I put aside My work, what seemed to be the greatest work, the work of saving souls, to seek to be in communion with My Father. Don't you think I knew that many people in the crowd I left behind were there out of nothing more than idle curiosity? Don't you think I knew that there must not be a race into the Kingdom? That it was not the shouting of a mob, but the still, small voice (1 Kings 19:11–12 NKJV) that would alone persuade men that I was the Son of God?

Why be surrounded by crowds if they did not really want to learn from and follow Me? Follow Me, the Christ, into the quiet places of prayer.

DECEMBER 10
THE QUIET TIME

There may be many times when I reveal nothing, command nothing, give no guidance. But your path is clear. And your task is also clear: to grow to know Me more and more each day. This quiet time with Me will enable you to do that.

I may ask you to sit silently before Me, and I may not speak any words that you could write down. Just the same, that waiting with Me will bring comfort and peace. Only friends who understand each other and love each other can wait silently in each other's presence.

And it may be that I shall demonstrate our friendship by asking you to wait in silence while I rest with you, assured of your love and understanding. So wait. So love. So rejoice!

DECEMBER 11
A SUNRISE GIFT

There are those whose lives have been full of stress and struggle, who have felt, as both of you have, the tragedy of living, the agony of a heart which breaks for My poor world. I give those followers of Mine that peace and joy which bring to the aging a second spring, the youth they sacrificed for Me and for My world …

Receive each day now as a joyous sunrise gift from Me. Doing your simple, daily tasks in My strength and love will reveal all of your highest hopes. Expect great things. Expect great things!

DECEMBER 12
CAREFREE

"Perfect love casts out fear."
(1 JOHN 4:18A NKJV)

Love and fear cannot live together. By their very natures, they cannot exist side by side. Evil is powerful, and fear is one of evil's strongest forces.

Therefore, a weak, indecisive love can soon be crushed by fear, whereas a perfect love, a trusting love, conquers immediately and fear, defeated, flees in confusion.

But I am love because God is love (1 John 4:8) and "I and My Father are one" (John 10:30 NKJV). So the only way to obtain this perfect love that drives away fear is to have Me in your lives more and more. You can only banish fear by My presence and by My name.

Fear of the future — Jesus will be with us.

Fear of poverty — Jesus will provide.

Every other temptation to fear — Jesus is the answer.

You must not allow fear to enter. Talk to Me. Think about Me. Talk about Me. Love Me. And that sense of My power will so take hold of you that no fear can take hold of your mind. Be strong in My love.

DECEMBER 13
CONTINUOUS GUIDANCE

Abundant joy. The joy of continuous guidance. The joy of knowing that every detail of your lives is planned by Me, but planned with a wealth of tenderness and love.

Wait for My guidance in every step. Wait to be shown My way. The thought of My leading you so lovingly should give you great joy. All of the responsibility of life is taken off your shoulders. All of its busyness and worry taken off your shoulders. It is indeed a joy for you to feel so free, and yet so planned for.

Oh! The wonder of this, a God-guided life. If there are any circumstances in which you think anything is impossible, you are saying it cannot be done by Me. To say that is truly a denial of Me.

DECEMBER 14
STORMS

Our loving Lord, we thank You for
Your marvelous keeping power.

There is no miracle as wonderful as the miracle of a soul being kept by My power (1 Peter 1:3–5). Forces of evil attack and assault, but they are powerless. Storms rage futilely.

It is like a cool garden with sweet flowers and bees and butterflies and trees and splashing fountains set in the middle of a huge, noisy city. Try to see your lives as being like that.

Seeing them not only as calm and stable, but as breathing sweet fragrance, expressing beauty. Expect storms (John 16:33). But know this — the two of you cannot be united in your great friendship and commitment to do My work, and in your great love for Me, and not provoke the envy, hatred, and hostility of everyone you meet who is not on My side.

Where does the enemy attack? The fortress, the strong tower, not the desert wasteland.

DECEMBER 15
MY SHADOW

Learn that each day must be lived in My power, and in the awareness of My presence, even if the thrill of joy seems to be absent. If there sometimes seems to be a shadow on your lives, remember that it is not the withdrawal of My presence. It is My shadow as I stand between you and your enemies.

There are quiet days even with those who are nearest and dearest to you. You do not doubt *their* love because you do not hear their laughter, and do not feel the thrill of joy you experience when they are with you.

The quiet, gray days are the days for you to do your duty. Work in the calm assurance that I am with you.

DECEMBER 16
WHAT JOY IS

Lord, give us Your joy, that joy no
man, no poverty, no circumstances,
and no conditions can take from us
(see John 16:22).

You shall have My joy. But just for now, life for both of you is a march — a strenuous march ... The joy will come, but do not think about that right now. Simply think of the march. Joy is the reward ...

Between My promising the gift of joy to My disciples and their realization of that joy came a sense of failure, disappointment, denial, desertion, and hopelessness. But then came hope, eager anticipation, and courage in the face of danger.

Joy is the reward for patiently seeing Me in the dull, dark days, when you trust Me even when you cannot see Me. Joy is, so to speak, your heart's response to My smile in recognition of your faithfulness …

Stop thinking everything in your lives is all wrong if you do not feel the joy … Remember, you may not be joyful yet, but you are brave. And courage and thinking unselfishly about others are as surely signs of true discipleship as is joy.

DECEMBER 17
CONDITIONS OF BLESSING

Jesus, we love You. We see that all things are planned by You. We rejoice in that vision.

Rejoice in the fact that you are Mine. The members of My kingdom have many privileges. When I said about My Father that "He makes His sun rise on the evil and on the good, and sends rain on the just and on the unjust" (Matthew 5:45b

NKJV), you will notice that I was speaking about worldly and material blessings.

I did not mean that the believer and unbeliever could be treated alike. That is not possible. I can send rain and sunshine, and money and worldly blessings equally to both, but that is impossible when it comes to the blessings of the kingdom.

There are conditions which control the giving of these blessings. My followers do not always understand this. But in order for them to understand, it is necessary for them to remember that after I said "He causes his sun to rise on the evil and the good ..."; I gave them My command — "Be perfect, therefore, as your heavenly Father is perfect" (Matthew 5:45, 48 NIV 1984).

It would be impossible for you to give your love and understanding, or exchange ideas with everyone equally. But you, too, should give material blessings just as My Father does. Everything must be done in love and in the spirit of true forgiveness.

DECEMBER 18
SEE WONDERS

Let your thoughts and meditations lead you into the very heart of My kingdom. There, see the abundance of delights in My storehouse, and take hold of them with joy.

See wonders, ask for wonders, carry wonders away with you. Remember, this beautiful earth on which you find yourself was once merely a thought in My divine mind. Consider how your thoughts could cause your corner of the earth to grow and become the Lord's garden. It can be like the home of Lazarus, Martha, and Mary in Bethany: a home for your Master, a place where I have the right to bring My friends, My children in need, so they can talk and rest with Me.

DECEMBER 19
PERFECT LOVE

Our Lord, give us that perfect love of You
that casts out all fear (see 1 John 4:18).

Never let yourselves fear anybody or anything. No fear of My failing you. No fear that your faith will fail you. No fear of poverty or loneliness. No fear of not knowing the way. No fear of others. No fear of their misunderstanding.

But, My children, this complete casting out of fear is the result of a perfect love, a perfect love of Me and My Father. Speak to Me about everything. Listen to Me at all times. Feel My tender nearness, and when any fear arises, immediately substitute it with some thought about Me.

The powers of evil watch you like an invading army would watch a guarded city—the objective always being to find some weak spot, attack it, and make a way to enter. This is how evil prowls around you, and seeks to surprise you with some fear or another.

The fear may have been only a small one, but it gives evil a weak spot to attack and then gain entrance. And then depression, doubt of Me, and so many other sins come rushing in. Pray, My beloved children, for that perfect love of Me that indeed casts out all fear.

DECEMBER 20
FIGHT DEPRESSION

Fight fear as you would fight a plague. Fight it in My name … Fear, even the smallest fear, hacks at the cords of love that bind you to Me.

However small a mark is made, in time those cords will wear thin, and then with one shock or disappointment, the cords snap. Without the little fears, the cords of love would have held.

Fight fear.

Depression is a state of fear. Fight that, too. Fight. Fight. Depression is the mark left by fear. Fight and conquer. Oh, fight and love and win, out of your love for Me and for the sake of My tender, never-failing love for you.

DECEMBER 21
SMILE INDULGENTLY

Children, regard every moment as one planned and arranged by Me. Remember, your Master is the Lord of every little thing that happens in the day. In every small thing, yield to My gentle pressure on your arm. Stay or go as that pressure — love's pressure — indicates.

I am the Lord of the moments, Creator of the snowflake and the mighty oak. More tender with the snowflake than the oak.

And when things do not turn out according to your plan, smile at Me indulgently. Smile with love and say to Me, as you would say to a loved one, "Have your way then" — knowing that My loving response will be to make the way as easy for you as it can be.

DECEMBER 22
MY PROTECTION

Fear no evil because I have conquered evil. Evil only has power to hurt those who do not place themselves under My protection. This is not a question of feelings; it is an assured fact.

All you have to do is say with assurance that whatever is attacking you cannot harm you because I have conquered it. Children, be assured of My conquering power, not only in the big things of life, but in the little things, too. Know that all is well. Be sure of it. Make it a habit. Learn it so well that it becomes automatic and instinctive for you.

But make it a habit in the smallest things, and then you will find you will do it easily, naturally, lovingly, and trustingly in the big things of life.

DECEMBER 23
THE WORLD'S SONG

Bless us O Lord, we beg You, and show us
the way in which You would have us walk
(see Psalm 143:8b).

Walk with Me in the way of peace. Spread peace, not strife, wherever you go. But it must be *My* peace.

Never a peace which is a truce with the power of evil. Never harmony if that means your life-music must be adapted to the mood and music of the world.

So often My disciples make the mistake of thinking that everything must be harmonious. No! Not when it means singing the world's song.

I, the Prince of Peace, said that "I did not come to bring peace, but a sword" (Matthew 10:34b NIV 1984).

DECEMBER 24
HE IS COMING

*Our Lord, You are here. Let
us feel Your closeness.*

Yes, I am coming. But remember, I must first be greeted the way the Magi greeted Me at the stable in Bethlehem. You must not greet Me at first as King and Lord in heavenly triumph, but as one of the lowliest, without any pageantry, as the Magi did.

The first greeting must be to the humble, the baby of Bethlehem. And to the humble, you must bring the worship of humility.

Then, the worship of repentance. As a sinner, you stand beside Me in the Jordan River, baptized by John (Matthew 3:13–17), worshiping Me as the friend and servant of sinners.

Think about My life often. Walk with Me. Share with Me. Humility, service, worship, sacrifice, sanctification — these are all steps in the Christian life.

DECEMBER 25
BABY OF BETHLEHEM

Kneel before the baby of Bethlehem. Accept the truth that the kingdom of heaven is for the lowly, the simple.

Bring to Me, the Christ-child, your gifts, truly the gifts chosen by the wisest men on earth.

Gold — your money.

Frankincense — the adoration of a life set apart for Me.

Myrrh — your sharing in My sorrows and those of the world.

"They presented gifts to Him: gold, frankincense, and myrrh" (Matthew 2:11b NKJV).

DECEMBER 26
HEALTH AND WEALTH

Don't be afraid. Health and wealth are coming to you both. My wealth is sufficient to meet your needs, and to enable you to do My work which you long to do.

Some people call wealth "money." And you know that having money to hoard and to flaunt is not for My disciples.

Travel through this world simply seeking the resources to do My will and My work. Never keep anything you are not using. Remember, everything I give you belongs to Me, and it is only given to you to use. Can you ever imagine Me hoarding My treasures? You must never hoard anything. Rely on Me.

To store up for the future is to *fear* and to doubt Me. Squelch every doubt of Me at once. Live in the joy of My constant presence. Yield every moment to Me. Perform every task, no matter how humble, as one I have gently called you to. Do them for Me, out of your love for Me. So live, so love, so work.

You are the apostles of the little services.

DECEMBER 27
GLORIOUS WORK

I have taken so much away from you, so that yours would truly be a life of well-being. Build, stone by stone, upon a rock (Matthew 7:24–27), a firm foundation. And that rock is your Master. That rock is Christ.

A life of discipline and of joyous fulfillment will be yours ... Never lose sight of the glorious work to which you have been called.

Do not let any riches or comforts tempt you to leave the path on which your feet have been set: the path of working miracles with Me. Love and laugh. Trust and pray. Ride on now in loving humility to victory.

DECEMBER 28
SIGNS AND FEELINGS

Our Lord, You are here. Let us
feel Your closeness.

I am here. Do not need "feeling" too much. To ask for "feeling" too often is the same as asking for a sign. And then the answer will be the same as the answer I gave while I was on earth. "A wicked and adulterous generation asks for a sign! But none will be given it except the sign of the prophet Jonah. For as Jonah was three days and three nights in the belly of a huge fish, so the Son of Man will be three days and three nights in the heart of the earth" (Matthew 12:39–40 NIV 2011).

Veiled from sight to the unbeliever (2 Corinthians 3:7–18). To the believer, the veiling is only temporary to be followed by a glorious resurrection ...

What difference does it make what you feel? What matters is what I am, was, and ever shall be to you — a risen Lord ... The *feeling* that I am with you may depend upon your mood at the moment, upon a change of circumstances, upon some trivial thing.

I am not influenced by circumstances ... When My promise is given, it is kept. I am here, one with you in tender, loving friendship.

DECEMBER 29
WORK AND PRAYER

Work and prayer represent the two forces that will ensure your success. Your work and My work.

For prayer, believing prayer, is based on the certainty that *I* am working for you and with you and in you.

Go forward gladly and unafraid. I am with you. With man, your task may be impossible, but with God, all things are possible (Matthew 19:26).

DECEMBER 30
FISHERS OF MEN

When you consider the people you read about who are in anguish, do you ever consider how My heart must ache with the sadness of it, with the agony of it?

If I saw the city of Jerusalem and wept over it (Luke 19:41), don't you think I would weep even more over the anguish of those troubled hearts, over the lives of people who try to live without My sustaining power?

"But [they] are not willing to come to Me that [they] may have life" (John 5:40 NKJV).

Live to bring others to *Me*, the only source of happiness and peace of heart.

DECEMBER 31
JESUS THE CONQUEROR

Jesus. That is the name by which you conquer. Jesus. Say My name, Jesus, not as cringing beggars, but like people calling out when they recognize a friend. "You shall call His name JESUS, for

He will save His people from their sins" (Matthew 1:21 NKJV).

And do not read "sins" only as vice and degradation, but also as doubts, fears, tempers, despair, impatience, and lack of love in the big and little things. Jesus. "He will save His people from their sins." Simply saying My name lifts the soul away from petty valley irritations to mountain heights.

"He will save His people from their sins." Savior and friend; joy-bringer and rescuer, leader and guide — Jesus. Do you need to be delivered from cowardice, adverse circumstances, from poverty, from failure, from weakness?

"There is no other name under heaven given to men by which we must be saved" (Acts 4:12b NIV 1984) — *Jesus*. Say it often. Claim the power it brings!

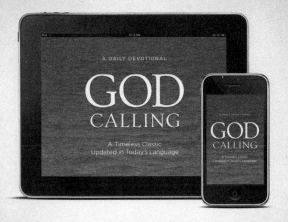